Family Walks in South Derbyshire

Gordon Ottewell

Scarthin Books of Cromford
Derbyshire
1993

Family Walks in South Derbyshire

General Editor: Norman Taylor

The Country Code

Respect the life and work of the countryside
Guard against all risk of fire
Fasten all gates
Keep your dogs under close control
Keep to public paths across farmland
Use gates and stiles to cross fences, hedges and walls
Leave livestock, crops and machinery alone
Take your litter home
Help to keep all water clean
Protect wildlife, plants and trees
Take special care on country roads
Make no unnecessary noise

Walking the routes in this book

All the routes in this book have been walked, in most cases, several times prior to publication and we have taken great care to ensure that they are on rights of way. However, changes occur all the time in the landscape; should you meet any obstructions, please let us know. Serious obstructions can be brought to the attention of the local branch of the Ramblers Association and the Rights of Way section of the County Council.

Published by Scarthin Books of Cromford, Derbyshire 1993

Printed in Great Britain at The Alden Press, Oxford

ISBN 0907758 614

Cover illustration by Andrew Ravenwood: Somersal Herbert Hall (Route 6)

The Alport Stone (Route 1)

Dedication

To Bill Cresswell, whose love for Derbyshire is infectious

Preface

Like many other Derbyshire exiles, I am always on the lookout for excuses to visit my native county and this book has provided a perfect reason for coming back again – and again!

I have on my desk before me a tattered copy of Jack Helyer's *Rambling in Derbyshire*, a book to which I owe a great deal. It was through the chance purchase of this book that my future wife and I began our journeys of discovery into our lovely county many years ago. I worked in coalmines then and this book not only widened my horizons but also got me out into the healthy Derbyshire air. A belated but sincere 'Thank you', Mr Helyer!

And now to this book. With the Peak District already well covered in the 'Family Walks' series, the demarcation of the scope of this, the third Derbyshire book, has been a difficult one to resolve, as has the choice of title. Where does south Derbyshire begin? Drawing arbitary lines on a map is asking for trouble so instead I have settled for a scatter of routes extending from the Trent Valley northwards as far as Alport Height and Carsington Water in the west and Shipley Country Park in the east.

To say I've enjoyed walking in these old haunts once more is a monumental understatement; may you find similar delight in doing so too.

Acknowledgements

I should like to thank Philip, Angela, Ben, Edward and Hannah Cope for so readily agreeing to act as guinea pigs during the preparation of this book.

I must also record my indebtedness to the various members of staff at the country parks, libraries and tourist information centres throughout the region for all their assistance, given with unfailing patience and cheerfulness.

Last, but by no means least, I wish to acknowledge the authors, too numerous to mention individually, whose books on Derbyshire have been invaluable to me. Many of their works have been on my shelves since my Derbyshire days; others I have added since. All have helped me to retain my affection for and knowledge of my native county.

Contents

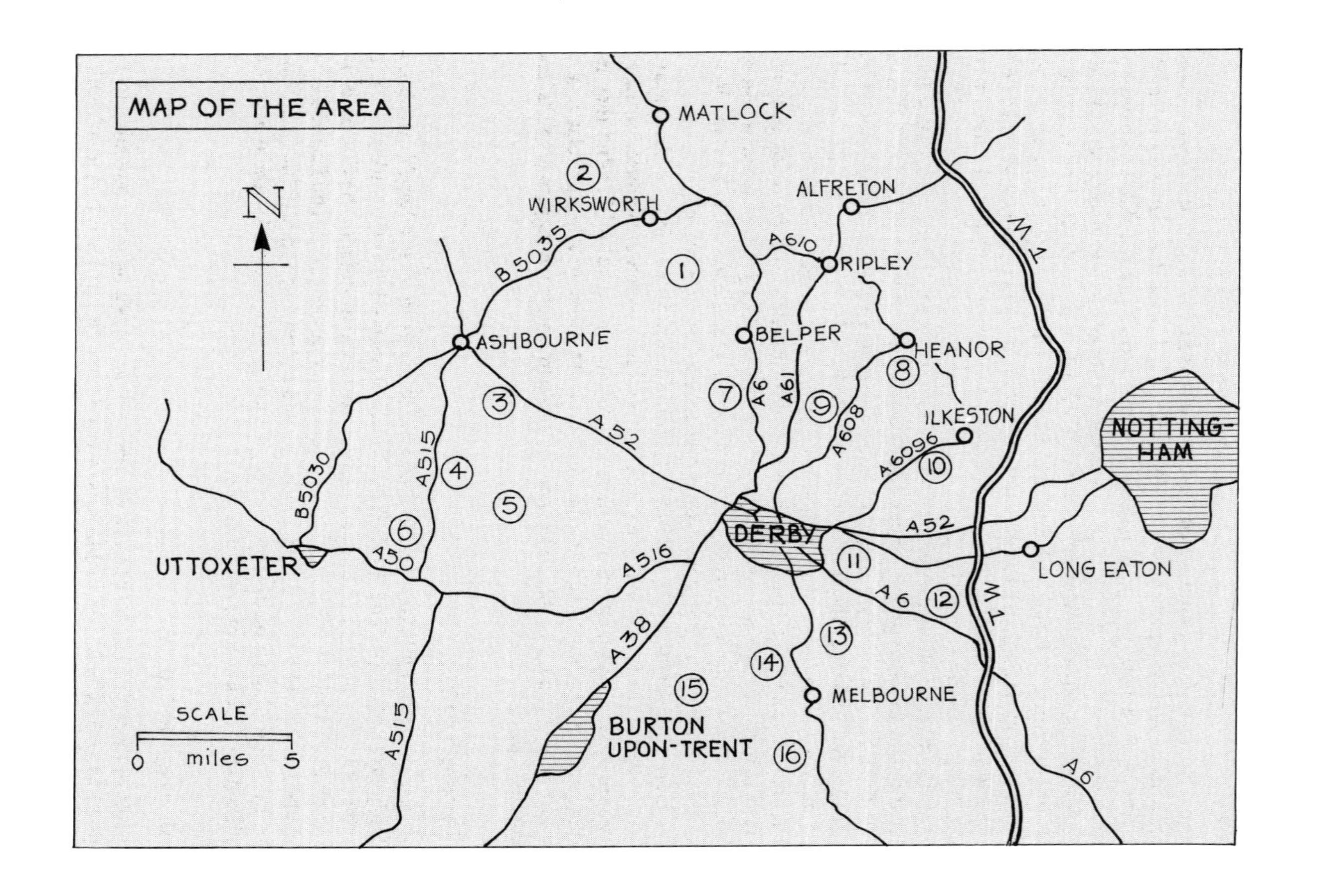

MAP OF THE AREA
N
MATLOCK
2
WIRKSWORTH
ALFRETON
B 5035
A610
RIPLEY
1
M1
ASHBOURNE
BELPER
HEANOR
8
3
7
A6
A61
9
A608
ILKESTON
A52
A6096
NOTTING-
HAM
B5030
A515
4
10
5
DERBY
A52
6
11
UTTOXETER
A50
A516
LONG EATON
A6
12
M1
13
A38
14
15
MELBOURNE
SCALE
0
miles
5
A515
BURTON
UPON-TRENT
16
A6

Introduction

Amazing though it sounds, that part of Derbyshire south of the Peak District remains to many people a largely undiscovered land. True, the scenery south of the Matlock area lacks the grandeur of the northern hills, the dales give way to meandering brooks and rivers picking their way through a gentler landscape, and mellow brick replaces weathered stone in the villages. And yet, here is peace, a wealth of natural history, and innumerable links with both our ancient and recent historical past. All these delights, and many more, await the family prepared to step out and see south Derbyshire for themselves, and this book is intended to help make this happy exploration possible.

Here then, are sixteen circular walks, ranging in length from 2 to 7 miles, their locations scattered across the countryside south of the Derbyshire Dales. Just as the lengths of the walks vary, so inevitably do the demands made on the walkers. This is because the region covered is a mixture of hills, valleys, and comparatively flat country, each with its own distinctive appeal. As the chief aim is to encourage children to enjoy the open air, the routes are planned with their interests and stamina in mind. Sometimes there is a pub or teashop along the route and whenever possible the more strenuous sections of the walk are tackled near the start. Road walking and retracing of steps are kept to an absolute minimum.

Under the heading 'Attractions', attention is drawn to some of the features along the route that are likely to appeal to children. Boredom-induced tiredness seldom arises if youngsters are interested and actively involved in what they are doing; an unusual sighting, a snippet of colourful history, or a legend related at an appropriate point on the route can often help to revive flagging spirits and enthusiasm.

Choosing a walk

Unless the children taking part are experienced walkers, it is advisable to choose fairly easy walks first. The appendix at the end of the book lists the walks in order of difficulty and reference to this will help to avoid the mistake of making excessive demands on children's keenness and stamina. In any case, most children relish the challenge of tackling more strenuous walks later. With very young children, it may be best to walk part of the route to begin with, or to arrange for the party to be picked up at some point on the route.

Allowing sufficient time

Most of the walks are intended as the best part of a day's outing, allowing time for play, exploring and rest stops. It is better to over-estimate rather than under-estimate the time required; there is nothing worse than having to route-march the last stages of the walk. As a rough guide, allow a pace of around a mile per hour for very young children, graduating to two miles per hour for the experienced ten-year-old.

What to wear

With a fickle climate like ours, go walking prepared for the worst! Sturdy, comfortable shoes are preferable to wellies, which can tire and chafe. Waterproof outer-garments, such as cagoules, are essential, while underneath, several layers of thin jumpers are better than one thick garment, as they allow more flexibility when weather conditions change. Headgear – caps and bobble-hats – should not be overlooked. And don't forget a roomy rucksack in which to carry food and drink, spare clothes, maps, guides, and so on.

Finding – and following – the way

Much of the walking in this book is along waymarked public footpaths and bridleways and with careful reference to both route directions and accompanying sketch maps, there is little danger of getting lost! Even so, it is a good idea to take along the Ordnance Survey Landranger sheet referred to under the heading 'Start', above the route directions for each walk. The routes can be found on 3 sheets, as follows:

119 – Buxton, Matlock and Dovedale
128 – Derby and Burton-on-Trent area
129 – Nottingham and Loughborough area

Occasionally, especially after a summer's growth, some stiles become overgrown and footpaths obscured or even blocked. At such times, a stout walking stick can be useful to clear the way. Farming operations, too, can result in paths being ploughed up or in other ways becoming difficult to find or follow, although most farmers do their best to keep the paths clear. Remember though, that this is an intensively farmed area, with arable farming accounting for a good deal of the land use. By law, a farmer has 14 days in which to make good a footpath after ploughing it up and county councils are taking steps to implement this requirement. If the worst comes to the worst, and the path proves impossible to follow, take the shortest detour round the edge of the field to regain the route. The presence of a bull on or near a public-right-of-way can be disconcerting to walkers. The law allows farmers to graze young bulls, and those defined as not belonging to one of the recognized dairy breeds, on or near paths, providing that they are accompanied by cows or heifers.

Refreshments

Although there are pubs on or near several of the routes, and most admit children, there is no guarantee that meals are provided. Remember too, that opening hours vary and some pubs are closed (for meals at least) on one day of the week. Family picnics involve some carrying – (lighter after the meal!) – but win hands-down for flexibility, economy and fun!

Shardlow Basin (Route 12)

About the author

Born and bred in Derbyshire, at Swanwick, Gordon Ottewell worked as a colliery surveyor in the Alfreton area for ten years before becoming a teacher. After service in schools at Alvaston and Darley Dale, he became headteacher of a village school in Oxfordshire and now lives at Winchcombe, in the Gloucestershire Cotswolds. His first book, *Journey from Darkness*, was set in Victorian Derbyshire.

His other books include:
Family Walks in the Cotswolds (Scarthin Books)
Family Walks in South Gloucestershire (Scarthin Books)
Family Walks in Hereford and Worcester (Scarthin Books)
Family Walks around Stratford and Banbury (Scarthin Books)
Warde Fowler's Countryside (Edited) (Severn House)
A Cotswold Country Diary (Barn Owl Books)
Gloucestershire Countryside (Minton & Minton)

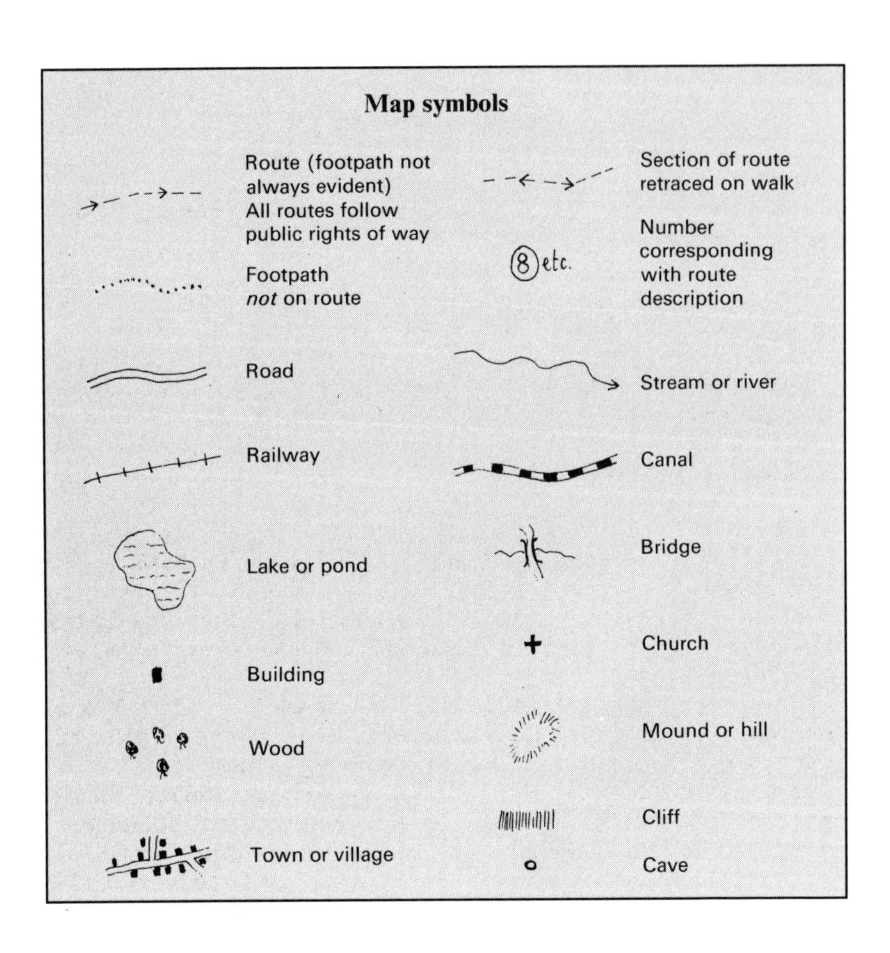
Map symbols
Route (footpath not always evident) All routes follow public rights of way
Section of route retraced on walk
Number corresponding with route description
8 etc.
Footpath *not* on route
Road
Stream or river
Railway
Canal
Lake or pond
Bridge
Church
Building
Mound or hill
Wood
Cliff
Town or village
Cave

Lapwing

Route 1 **$3\frac{1}{2}$ miles**

Around Alport Height

Outline

Alport Height car park – Broadgates – Lane End – Lawn Farm – Spout – Alport Height car park.

Summary

A short walk of gentle climbs and descents, along public footpaths and minor roads. As the sketch map shows, the route can be shortened by using more of the network of paths for which the area is noted but as the narrow winding lanes are so delightful and comparatively traffic-free, little advantage is gained by 'cutting corners' in this way. The views throughout are pleasant, though the most impressive is of course from Alport Height itself.

Attractions

Rising to 314 metres (1034 feet) above sea level, Alport Height (or Hill as it is sometimes called) is the most southerly hill of over 1000 feet in Derbyshire. Although outside the Peak District, it is an impressive landmark and the aerial masts of the Derbyshire County Police crowning its summit are visible from many miles distant.

The nine-acre hilltop was presented to the National Trust in 1930 and it commands a vast scenic panorama, extending on a clear day as far as the Wrekin and the Clee Hills of Shropshire, a distance of some 50 miles.

Just below the summit, in the hollow formed by old quarry workings, stands the Alport Stone, a massive gritstone monolith that has long attracted rock-climbers to pit their skills against its jagged form. Millstone grit is a coarse-grained sandstone rock which forms the bedrock of the so-called Dark Peak and of much of the Pennines. Alport Stone is the first example of a large block of this rock to be encountered by travellers from the south.

Near to the stone is a guidepost, also of millstone grit, bearing the quaintly-spelt names Ash-born, Darby and Wirksworth, and the date 1710. This once stood at a nearby road junction but was then replaced and used as a gatepost until it was re-erected here.

This open hilltop makes an excellent playground and picnic place. Scrambling over its humps and hollows provides endless fun and there is also plenty of scope for wildlife watching. The bright yellow of the prickly gorse bushes adds a welcome touch of colour and as the shrub is in flower for the greater part of the year, this has given rise to the saying:

> 'When gorse is not in bloom,
> Then kissing is out of favour.'

Continued on page 14

Route 1

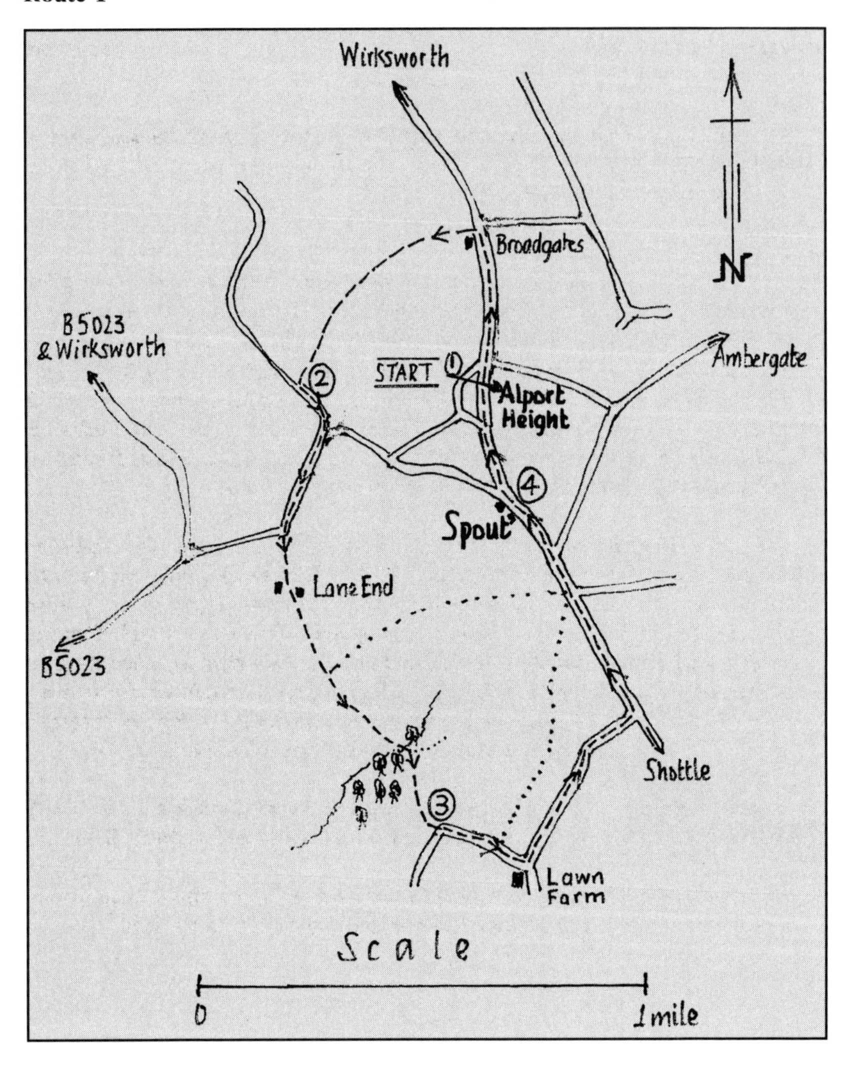
Wirksworth
Broadgates
N
B5023
& Wirksworth
START
Alport
Height
Ambergate
Spout
Lane End
B5023
Shottle
Lawn
Farm
Scale
0
1 mile

Route 1

Around Alport Height 3½ miles

Start

National Trust car park, Alport Height. Reached along unclassified roads from A517 via Shottle or by taking Alport road from B5035, ½ mile east of Wirksworth (OS Landranger Sheet 119. GR 304517).

Route

1. *From the car park, walk down to the road and turn right to reach a crossroads. Keep straight on along Alport Lane (i.e. following Wirksworth signpost). Beyond Broadgates Farm on the left, take the track, also on the left. Cross a cattle grid and instead of following the track as it swings left, keep straight on to pass through a gap-stile between a wall and a gate. The footpath keeps a hedge on the left as far as another gap-stile in the wall on the left. From now as far as the next road, white arrows on stiles indicate the route, which descends through 7 more stiles (the fifth of which bears the date 1870) to reach a narrow sloping road.*

2. *Turn left up this road to join the wider Alport-to-Wirksworth one. Turn right here and continue as far as a right-hand bend, at which point a lane branches off to the left. Follow this lane past houses, after which it becomes a grassy track which crosses a field via a stile by a gate to reach a gateway by a water trough. Continue straight on as far as a stile by a tree. From this point, bear right to follow the hedge on the right down a long field. Cross a stile at the bottom right hand corner and descend a winding track between trees and over a stream. At a fork, bear right to cross a stile by a gate and continue up the track to reach a road.*

3. *Turn left and continue to a T-junction by Lawn Farm. Turn left, following the Alport sign and left again at the next junction to reach the hamlet of Spout.*

4. *From here, turn right, following the Wirksworth signpost, up Alport Lane, passing Alport Stone on the right, to reach the car park approach on the right.*

Small finches such as linnets and goldfinches nest on gorse-covered hillsides and kestrels can often be seen hovering on outspread wings over the hill as they search for small mammals such as mice and voles. Incidentally, gorse has given its name to the hillside between Alport Height and Wirksworth, which is shown as Gorseybank on the Ordnance Survey map.

Talking of place-names, that of the hamlet of Spout, the only settlement of any size passed on the route, may lead to some speculation, as also may the nameplates indicating two lanes – Palace and Jubilee – also encountered on the way back to the car park.

Refreshments

There is no inn nearby, so why not enjoy a picnic high on this fine hilltop?

The kugel, Carsington Water visitor centre

Route 2 **$3\frac{3}{4}$ miles**

Carsington Water

Outline

Millfields car park – Hognaston – Uppertown – Visitor Centre – Millfields car park

Summary

This route combines a visit to Derbyshire's newest reservoir with a far-from-strenuous walk to the nearby village of Hognaston, much of it through newly-planted woodland. The one demanding uphill stretch, along the public footpath from below Hognaston chuch to Uppertown, is more than compensated for by the scenic descent to Carsington Water visitor centre, from which the final mile of the route follows the dam wall back to Millfields car park.

Attractions

Friday 22 May 1992 was both an exciting and important date in Derbyshire history. On that day, Her Majesty the Queen inaugurated Carsington Water, Derbyshire's – and Britain's – newest reservoir, a vast expanse of water that will almost certainly be the last to be opened in the 20th century.

A glance at an Ordnance Survey map published before that date shows the valley of the Scow Brook, between the villages of Carsington, Hognaston and Kirk Ireton, to be a sparsely populated area of fields, woods and scattered farms. Not any more. The damming of this valley by a 1200 metres-long embankment has created a huge reservoir covering almost 300 hectares (about 700 acres) with a maximum depth of 31 metres and a capacity of nearly 36,000 megalitres.

Plans for a new reservoir to supply the needs of the growing population of Derbyshire, Nottinghamshire and Leicestershire were made in the 1960s. In order to ensure that the minimum of damage was caused to the environment, over half a million trees and shrubs have been planted and nature conservation and study areas have been established on the Water itself. To encourage public interest, an excellent visitor centre has been built.

In addition, a wide range of water-sport activities are catered for. These include a sailing club, a canoeing, subaqua and windsurfing base, cycle hire and a children's playground, which is passed on the last stretch of the walk. Thousands of brown trout have been released into the Water to enable fishing to take place.

Carsington Water, in other words, is much more than just a reservoir. The visitor centre includes displays, working exhibits and interactive models showing how the reservoir fits into the local landscape and how the water stored here is piped to over 3 million customers as far afield as Derby, Nottingham and Leicester.

Whatever you do, don't miss seeing the kugel – a huge granite ball that spins at the slightest touch. How do you think it works?

Continued on page 18

Route 2

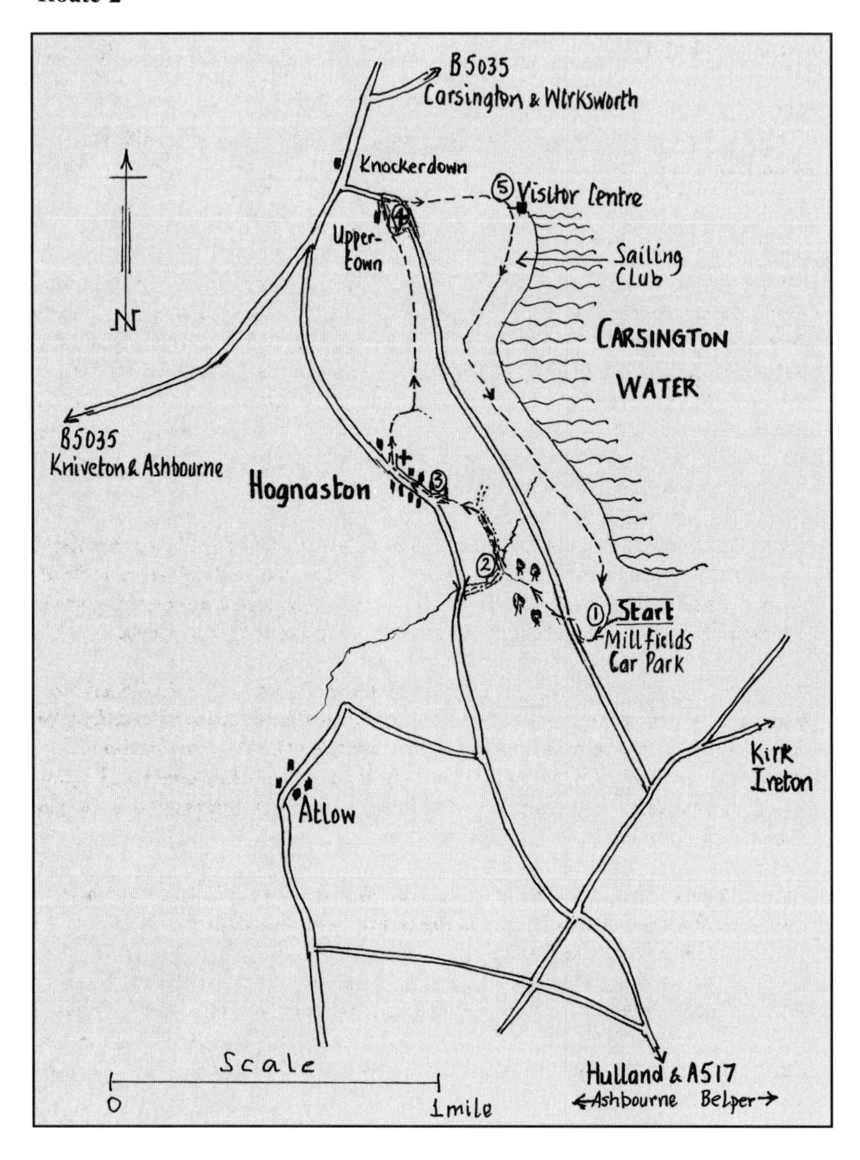
B5035
Carsington & Wirksworth
Knockerdown
5 Visitor Centre
4
Upper-town
Sailing Club
CARSINGTON
WATER
N
B5035
Kniveton & Ashbourne
Hognaston
3
2
1 Start
Mill Fields Car Park
Kirk Ireton
Atlow
Scale
0
1 mile
Hulland & A517
Ashbourne
Belper

Route 2

Carsington Water — $3\frac{3}{4}$ miles

Start

Millfields car park. Reached by following Carsington Water signs from Hulland Ward on A517 (Belper–Ashbourne road). Watch for sign on right indicating Millfields car park (OS Landranger Sheet 119. GR 246498).

Route

1. *Facing the reservoir from the toilet block, turn left along the obvious footpath. Cross the approach road and follow the gravel path. In 150 metres, as the path swings right, turn left to cross the road over stiles to follow a public footpath sign indicating Hognaston Bridge. The path soon dips, crossing 3 more stiles. Beyond the last of these it swings right. Follow the finger posts through newly planted woodland. Beyond the next stile, the path descends steeply before levelling out and leaving the woodland. Cross a stile straight ahead and go over a service road to descend a track and cross a footbridge to the left of a ford.*

2. *Climb the track as far as a right-hand bend. Here, go through the gate straight ahead, with a fence on the right initially. At the end of a second patch of woodland, the path veers right through a hedge gap and crosses 5 stiles, the last of which, in the left-hand corner of a field by a house, leads to Hognaston village street.*

3. *Turn right up the street, and go as far as St Bartholomew's church. Immediately beyond, turn right down a lane. At the foot, bear right, with cottages on the left, for 200 metres, as far as stepping stones over a stream, leading to a lane climbing to the left. At the lane end, continue on the same line through a stile by a gate and, keeping a hedge on the left, climb to a farm. Go through a stile by a gate to pass right of Uppertown Farm and reach a metalled lane.*

4. *Follow the lane towards the road ahead. Just before reaching it, turn right along a grassy path by a caravan site and cross the road to descend a track to the Carsington Water Visitor Centre.*

5. *Leave the Centre by aiming for the landward side of the sailing club. Signposts eventually indicate Millfields. Pass first a playground and then the sailing club on the left, before following the dam wall back to Millfields car park and the start.*

As with Derbyshire's other, well-established reservoirs, there is every sign that Carsington Water, together with its growing woodlands and the adjacent unspoilt countryside, will become an ideal site for nature-watching, especially birds. Already, mute swans, Canada geese and various species of wild duck have taken up residence here – watch this vast watery space for more exciting wildlife sightings.

Refreshments
Obtainable at the visitor centre, the Knockerdown Inn and the Red Lion Inn, Hognaston. Picnic facilities at the visitor centre and at Millfields car park.

Thatching at Osmaston

Route 3 **4½ miles**

Shirley and Osmaston

Outline

Shirley – Osmaston – Omaston Park – Park Lane – Shirley

Summary

This walk of gentle gradients is notable for the variety of scenery through which it passes. Leaving Shirley village, it follows public footpaths over fields at first, before entering woodland and climbing through the grounds of the demolished Osmaston Manor to reach the picturesque village of Osmaston. After providing good views of ornamental lakes, the return journey passes through more parkland to conclude along Park Lane, which leads back to Shirley.

Attractions

South of a line drawn between Ashbourne and Belper, the Derbyshire countryside takes on a distinctly different appearance from the hills-and-dales scenery of the popular northern region of the county. The rocky climbs and breathtaking views give way to an altogether gentler landscape of mellow red-brick villages surrounded by hedged fields, which together with expanses of well-wooded parkland, create a chequerwork countryside threaded by wriggling southward-flowing streams and brooks contributing their waters to the giant River Trent.

Shirley and Osmaston are neighbouring south Derbyshire villages. Each surrounded by parkland, they are linked by two footpaths and separated by the Shirley Brook, which after being dammed to form the lakes in Osmaston Park, continues its journey southwards to meet the Sutton Brook at Longford (see Route 5).

Villages set in parks were often the property of wealthy landowners, who sometimes planned the layout of the village and built the estate-workers' cottages to create a 'picturesque' effect. Osmaston is such a place. Although there was a village here centuries ago, much of what we see today is the work of Francis Wright, a Victorian ironworks proprietor, who built himself a fine Tudor-style mansion, planted trees and shrubberies, and created lakes by damming the Shirley Brook.

Osmaston Manor, as Wright's country house was called, was demolished some years ago. Now all that remains is the tower, which peeps over the trees. It is these trees – a splendid avenue of limes and some noble beeches – that, together with the lakes, enrich this walk. Both provide ideal habitat for bird life, the trees attracting nuthatches, blue, great and coal tits, while the lakes are popular with a host of waterfowl, including coot, mallard, little grebes and Canada geese. Even the ornamental pond on the green at the crossroads has its bird life – in this case domestic ducks which are only too ready to devour any food on offer!

Any time remaining can be put to good use on a walkabout around Shirley,

Continued on page 22

Route 3

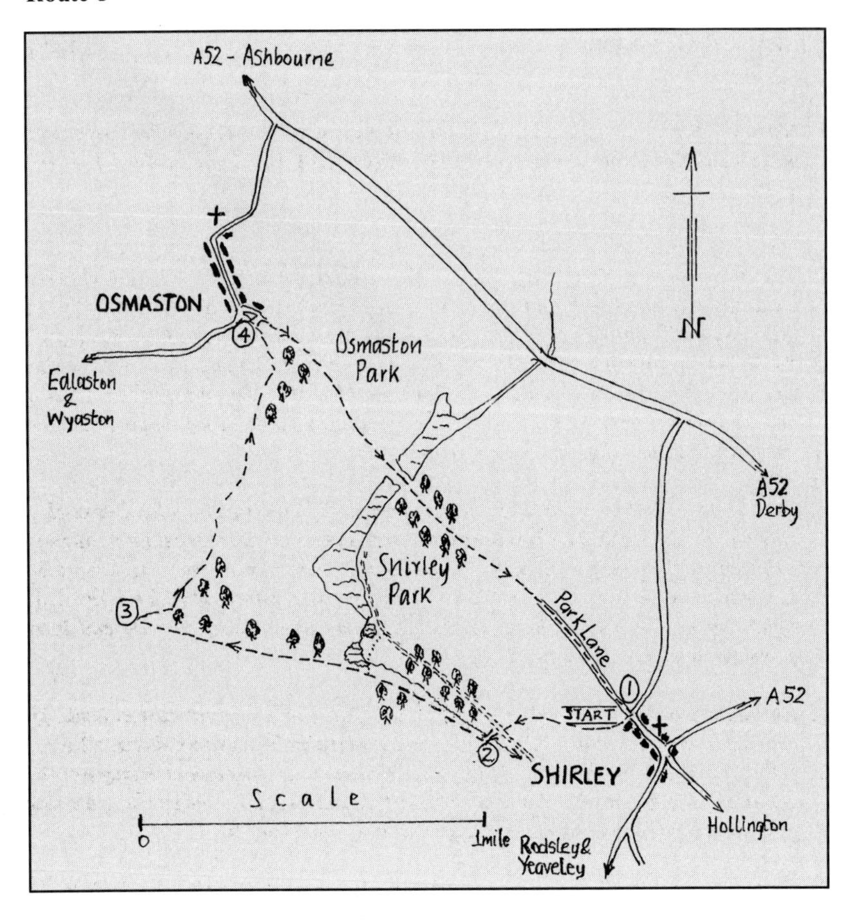

A52 - Ashbourne
OSMASTON
Osmaston Park
Edlaston & Wyaston
A52 Derby
Shirley Park
Park Lane
START
SHIRLEY
A52
Hollington
Rodsley & Yeaveley
Scale
0
1mile
N

Route 3

Shirley and Osmaston — $4\frac{1}{2}$ miles

Start

Shirley village. Shirley lies one mile south of the A52 (Derby–Ashbourne road) and $4\frac{1}{2}$ miles SE of Ashbourne. Park in the village (OS Landranger Sheet 128. GR 219417).

Route

1. *Pass the church and the old school on the right and continue to a road junction. Take the left-hand fork (no through road) and almost immediately turn left to follow a public footpath sign up steps and over 3 stiles into a field. Keep a hedge on the left and follow it as it swings right, down to a stile. Beyond, bear right, with a hedge now on the right, to enter a field over another stile. Leave over a further stile and turn left to descend, with a hedge on the left, to a stile by a handgate. Cross a track and continue over a footbridge and stile.*

2. *Turn right to follow the Shirley Brook, eventually entering woodland through a gateway on the right. The path winds through the trees before meeting a roughly-surfaced track coming in from the right. Follow it straight on, ignoring side paths. Leave the woodland through a stile by a gate and enter parkland with a lake on the right. Do not turn right here; instead, keep on along the lake side and later alongside woodland, crossing 3 stiles.*

3. *100 metres beyond the 3rd stile, where the fence on the right curves back, go through a gate adjoining and follow a woodland track. This passes through 2 gates before climbing to the left. After some distance, go through a handgate and continue through shrubberies and along a tree-lined road. After crossing a cattle grid, turn left to reach a green at a junction of roads and tracks.*

4. *To see Osmaston village, keep straight on. To return to Shirley, go back to the junction by the green and follow the lane signposted 'Bridle path to Shirley.' This clear path dips to pass between two lakes and then climbs through woodland before becoming a minor road for the last mile of its course back to the road junction from which the footpath section of the walk commenced.*

preferably making use of an excellent little guidebook, *Look at Shirley Village*, on sale in the church. This is specially designed to appeal to Junior-age children and is packed with information, as well as clues to encourage keen eyes and sharp minds. It also makes a worthwhile souvenir of the day's walk.

Refreshments
Saracen's Head Inn, Shirley. Shoulder of Mutton Inn, Osmaston.

Bentley Hall

Route 4 **$3\frac{1}{2}$ miles**

Cubley and Hungry Bentley

Outline

Cubley village – Cubley Common – Hungry Bentley – Coppice Farm – Cubley Church – Cubley village.

Summary

This is a short walk, chiefly along little-used footpaths, over gently rolling countryside rich in history. Waymarking, at the time the route was surveyed, left something to be desired but careful reading of the directions should ensure that families encounter no difficulties on this easy yet absorbing walk.

Attractions

The Ordnance Survey map shows two Cubleys – Great and Little – perched on a slope of the fertile undulating country between Ashbourne and Uttoxeter. Great Cubley was once important enough to be granted both a fair and a market, the latter being famous, according to an old book, for its fat hogs. Today, however, few people distinguish between the two Cubleys.

But if Cubley's story is one of decline, Hungry Bentley's is one of almost complete disappearance. Apart from Bentley Fields Farm and Bentley Hall, nothing remains of this ancient village except for a number of mounds and ditches in a field, which aerial photography has revealed to be the outlines of the cottages and streets of this long-abandoned settlement.

Why did the people of Hungry Bentley desert their village? This mystery is sure to give rise to some lively discussion as walkers pause to ponder after climbing up to the humps and hollows that mark the site of this lost village. Was plague the reason, or were the inhabitants driven away by some tyrannical landlord, determined to impose his will, say for the establishment of sheepwalks? Or does the key to the puzzle lie in the word 'Hungry', denoting perhaps that despite its apparently well-chosen site, Hungry Bentley withered for lack of food, or water, or both?

By contrast, the nearby farmhouse of Bentley Hall has not only survived but done so in style. It is a splendidly ornate late-16th century building, well worth making the short detour to see.

Back at Cubley, another mystery awaits. Why did the fine mansion of the Montgomerys disappear, leaving only a mound and a remnant of the moat in the field opposite the church? Follow the Marston Montgomery signpost along the footpath and take a look at the site. Inside the church can be seen two sadly defaced tombs of 15th century Montgomerys, one of the armour-clad Sir Nicholas, who died in 1435, and the other of a later Sir Nicholas and his wife Joan, a once beautiful tomb with small figures carved into niches around the side of the tomb-chest and dating from 1494. Also in the church is a remarkably well written and illustrated history of Cubley and district, the work of a 12-year-old local girl.

Route 4

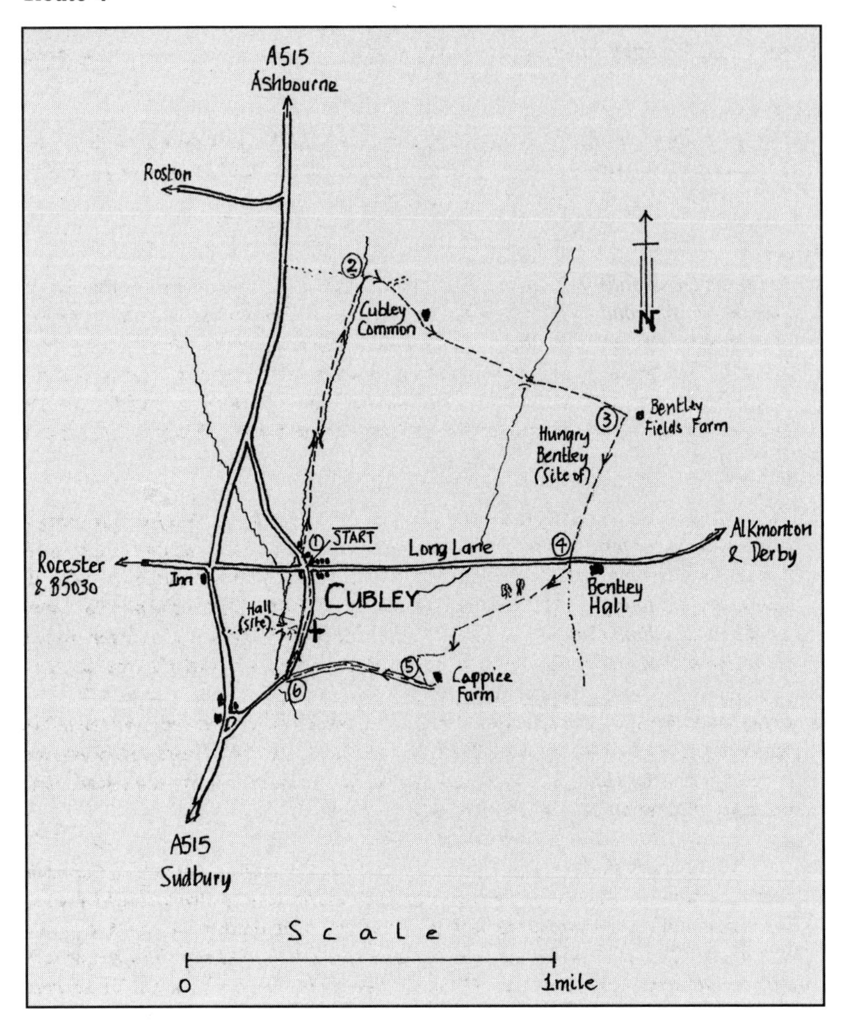
A515
Ashbourne
Roston
Cubley
Common
Bentley
Fields Farm
Hungry
Bentley
(Site of)
START
Long Lane
Alkmonton
& Derby
Rocester
& B5030
Inn
CUBLEY
Hall
(site)
Bentley
Hall
Coppice
Farm
A515
Sudbury
Scale
0
1mile

Route 4

Cubley and Hungry Bentley — $3\frac{1}{2}$ miles

Start

Cubley village. It lies ½ mile east of the A515, midway between Sudbury and Ashbourne. Park as near as possible to the crossroads in the centre of the village (OS Landranger Sheet 128. GR 162382).

Route

1. *From the crossroads, take the minor road opposite that is signposted to the church. Just before the road dips to the left, follow a public footpath sign to the right to a stile in the hedge straight ahead (ignoring a stile on the right). Walk alongside a brook with a hedge on the right, crossing another stile and going over a field and through a metal gate. Eventually the path crosses a footbridge and follows the opposite bank, crossing a stile and continuing to another, which gives access to a farm road.*

2. *Turn right, cross a cattle grid, and bear right at a fork. Just before reaching a farmhouse on the left, leave the road, turning left to pass a signpost and reach a stile in a hedge. Keeping another hedge on the right, descend a field and cross a double stile to enter a long field. Continue down to a brick footbridge at the bottom right-hand corner. Climb the slope ahead, between a hedge and a bank. At the top, with a farm ahead, cross a stile in a fence on the right to reach the site of Hungry Bentley.*

3. *Leave by making for a hedge corner straight ahead and keep the hedge on the left to pass through a gateway. Bentley Hall can now be seen ahead. Cross a field, aiming to the right of the Hall, to a stiled footbridge, beyond which keep on the same line, crossing another stile, to reach a road.*

4. *Turn left towards Bentley Hall. In 20 metres before the Hall is reached, the route passes through a gateway on the right. Instead of following the track ahead, cross a field diagonally right, passing left of an overgrown quarry to reach a gated footbridge. Beyond, pass left of a wood and cross a stile in a hedge. Go straight over a field and through a metal gate. Cross the next field diagonally left and then bear right between a fence and a hedge. The route now skirts Coppice Farm, passing through 3 metal gates before swinging left along a fence to reach the farm drive through the final gate.*

5. *Turn right and follow the drive to reach a road.*

6. *Turn right, passing Cubley church and hall site, back to the crossroads and the start.*

Refreshments
Howard Arms, Cubley (on A515).

Nearby attractions
Bentley Fields Open Farm. A working dairy farm with rare breeds. Play area. Field trail over Hungry Bentley village site. The birthplace of Samuel Johnson's father: a house by the A515 at Cubley Common bears a plaque to commemorate Dr Johnson's father, who later moved to Lichfield to set up as a bookseller. His son, the compiler of the first dictionary, was born there in 1709.

Longford Park

Route 5 **$2\frac{1}{4}$ miles**

Longford – A Village and its Park

Outline

Longford – Longford Park – Longford.

Summary

A short walk, level throughout, around one of south Derbyshire's most interesting villages, extended to include the adjacent parkland, with its hall, church, and farm buildings, rich in associations with one of the great pioneers of modern British agriculture.

Attractions

A family of experienced walkers could complete this short route without much effort in an hour or so and end up wondering how such an easy stroll found its way into a book of family walks, to the exclusion of longer, more demanding routes.

The chief reason for its inclusion – apart from the obvious one of providing at least one short, simple stroll, well within the capabilities of the most inexperienced youngster – is that there is more to the scattered village of Longford than at first meets the eye.

Someone once wrote that so many signposts point to Longford that it comes as something of a disappointment to find such a small, insignificant place. Well, we shall see. To start with, its name is worth thinking about. Longford grew up by the side of the old Roman road extending westwards from Little Chester (Derby) through Rocester and into Staffordshire. Along the unwaveringly straight stretch of this road to the east of the village is a hamlet called Long Lane. As Longford stood at the meeting place of two brooks, now bridged but in past times crossed by fords, its name could hardly be more apt.

Two interesting buildings face each other near the start of the walk. On the left stands the former water mill, a private residence now but still retaining telltale evidence of its original use. Opposite can be seen a low wooden building which, according to a plaque, was the first cheese factory built in England, having opened on 4 May 1870, under the management of one Cornelius Schermerhow!

It is the cluster of buildings in Longford Park, however, that provide the most fascinating ingredients of this walk. If the substantial farm buildings look impressive, then so they should, for the Longford estate belonged for over 300 years to the Coke family (pronounced Cook), one of whom, Thomas William, was better known as Coke of Holkham, one of the greatest agriculturists who ever lived.

Holkham is in Norfolk, and it was there that Coke popularised the growing of potatoes, improved crop rotation, brought in new farm machinery and introduced what we now call agricultural shows. But it was at Longford Hall that the great Coke spent his boyhood and where in 1842 he died, at the ripe old age of 88.

Continued on page 30

Route 5

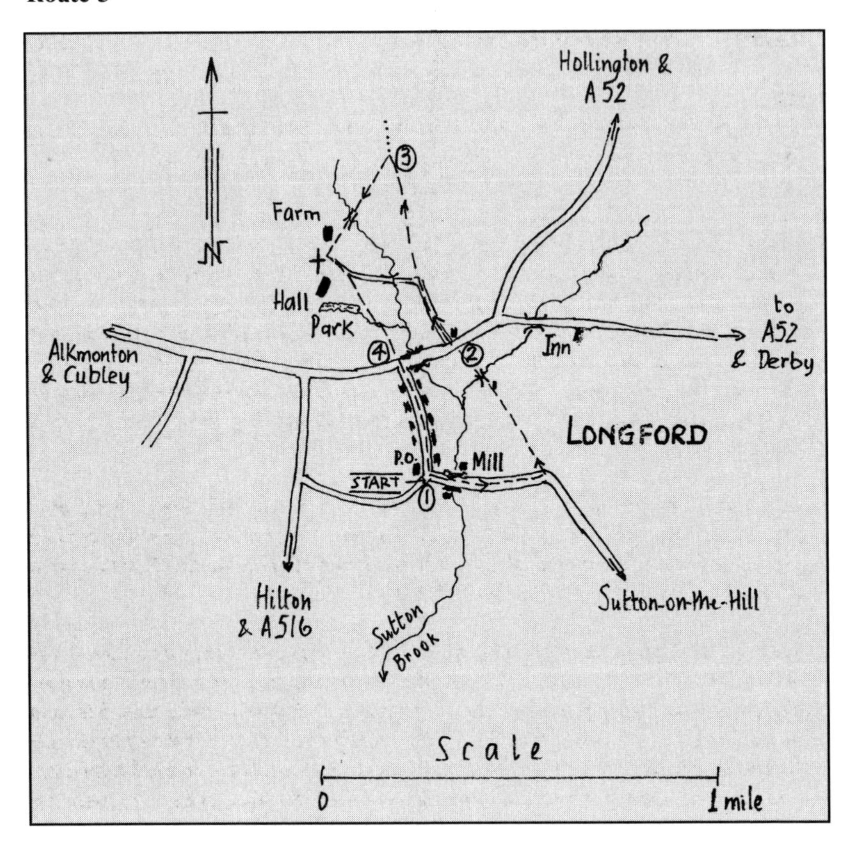

Grey squirrel

Route 5

Longford – A Village and its Park $2\frac{1}{4}$ miles

Start

Longford lies south of the A52 (Derby–Ashbourne road), 5 miles SW of Brailsford. Park in the village (OS Landranger Sheet 128. GR 220374).

Route

1. *From the road junction by the post office (and farm of the same name), follow the Sutton-on-the-Hill road over the bridge and past the converted water mill and former cheese factory opposite. At a right-hand bend, turn left to follow a public footpath sign indicating Shirley and Rodsley. Cross a field diagonally left to a stile by a gate alongside a cottage (yellow arrow). Continue over a metalled track to a stile opposite and keep a hedge on the right. Ignore a path and a footbridge (also on the right) and continue straight on to cross a gated footbridge and a field to reach a road.*

2. *Cross straight over and continue along a drive signposted Longford Church. Immediately before a left-hand bend, keep straight on through a handgate (blue arrow) to follow a straight path with a ditch and fence on the right. Pass through a gate to reach a junction of the path with a track.*

3. *Turn left and follow the track to pass through a farmyard. Leave by a metal gate opposite Longford church. To visit this interesting church, turn right and enter the churchyard through a gate on the left. From the church, go down the main drive and through a gate by a cattle grid. In 25 metres, where the fence on the right curves, turn right, crossing a drive leading to an ornamental gate. Go over a field and cross a footbridge. Turn left now to follow the brook for 100 metres before crossing a field to the right to reach a road junction through a gate.*

4. *Go straight over to return to the village, passing the school before reaching the road junction by the post office and the start.*

Although he was buried in Norfolk, a memorial bust can be seen in Longford church, together with an intriguing collection of other memorials representing the Longford and Coke families.

A brief glimpse can be had of the restored Tudor hall, and of the weirs built by the Cokes along the Shirley Brook, on the walk across the park back to the village.

Refreshments
Ostrich Inn, Longford.

Somersal Herbert Hall

Route 6 **7 miles**

Doveridge, Waldley and Somersal Herbert

Outline

Doveridge – Dove Bridge – Staffordshire Way – Waldley – Somersal Herbert – Doveridge.

Summary

A longer-than-usual walk, chiefly along little-used field paths, close to the Staffordshire border. A few of the waymark signs along the route were missing at the time of the survey, while others encountered indicated non-existent gaps in hedges! However, experienced family walkers should find this gently undulating walk in quiet if unspectacular countryside an enjoyable experience.

Attractions

The River Dove, no longer the clear limestone stream admired by thousands at Dovedale, dominates the first mile of this walk. Doveridge, Derbyshire's most south-westerly village, takes its name from the river, which is crossed by 3 contrasting bridges, the first of which is an elegant footbridge, the second the modern structure carrying the busy A50, and the third, the handsome old Dove Bridge, dated 1691, and now happily relegated to footbridge status.

At this point, the Dove receives the waters of the Tean, a tributary river flowing in from Staffordshire, while a few miles upstream, off the route, the River Churnet also helps to swell the growing Dove. Although the Dove forms the county boundary in this region, the route follows a short stretch of the Staffordshire Way, a 92-mile long-distance footpath.

After parting company with the Staffordshire Way, the route climbs steadily, passing a white-painted concrete pillar, standing at 157 metres (515 feet) above sea level. This is a trig. point, one of many fixed positions erected by the Ordnance Survey at commanding viewpoints and now, thanks to new surveying techniques, rapidly becoming redundant.

Well-planned walks usually keep something special for the closing stages and this one is no exception. Somersal Herbert is a tiny place but it boasts two precious possessions, an interesting and well-kept church and a beautiful timber-framed hall next door that dates from 1564 and is considered by many to be the finest Tudor house in Derbyshire.

Back at Doveridge, any remaining time can be spent visiting St Cuthbert's church, the churchyard of which is noted for its venerable yew tree, said to be centuries old. Several interesting monuments enrich this church, one of the most appealing of which represents William and Mary Davenport and their children, shown kneeling at prayer. The father is depicted in cavalier dress, the mother and daughters are clad in full-skirted gowns with lace-trimmed collars, and the baby of the family is shown peeping from a cradle.

Route 6

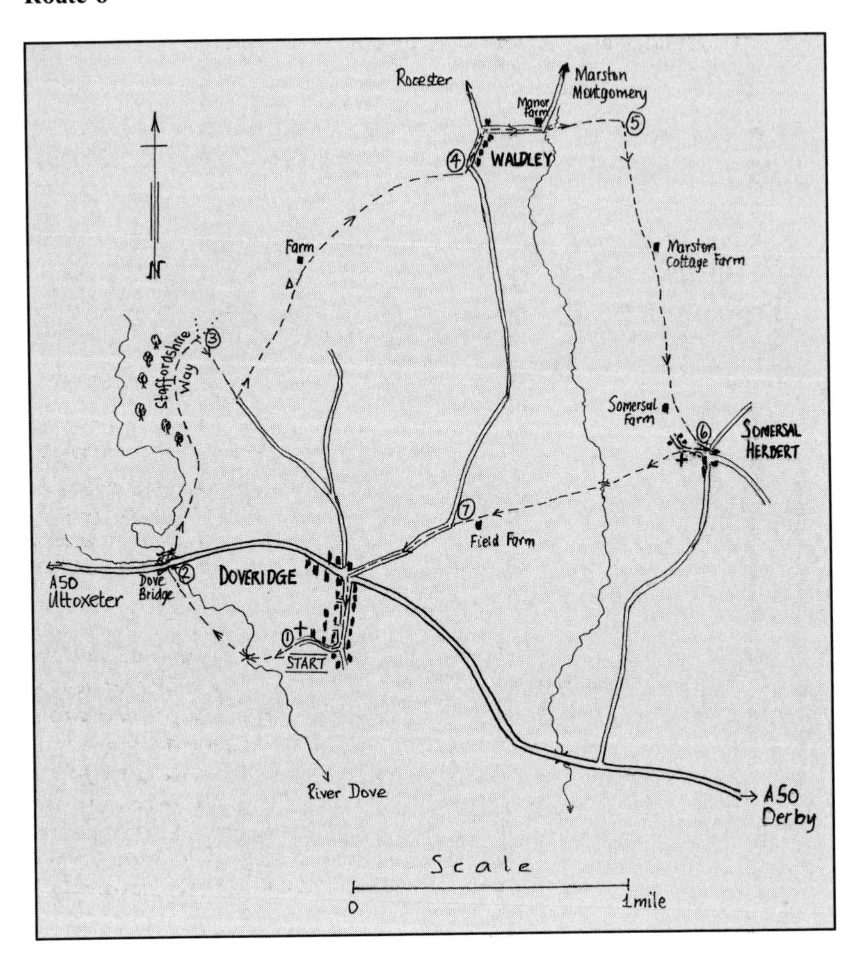
Rocester
Marston
Montgomery
Manor
Farm
5
4
WALDLEY
Farm
Marston
Cottage Farm
N
Staffordshire
Way
3
Somersal
Farm
6
SOMERSAL
HERBERT
7
Field Farm
A50
Uttoxeter
Dove
Bridge
2
DOVERIDGE
1
START
River Dove
A50
Derby
Scale
0
1mile

Route 6

Doveridge, Waldley and Somersal Herbert — 7 miles

Start

Doveridge, a village alongside the A50 (Stoke–Derby road) $2\frac{1}{2}$ miles east of Uttoxeter. Park on Church Lane, south of the A50 (OS Landranger Sheet 128. GR 114341).

Route

1. *Walk down the lane and past the church. Beyond a layby on the left, follow a public footpath sign between wire fences. Cross a footbridge and a suspension bridge over the River Dove and follow the causeway path over a third footbridge to reach the A50 over a stile at a new bridge.*

2. ***Cross this busy road with extreme care** and turn right. In 20 metres, turn left to reach the old Dove Bridge by steps. Cross and descend a bank to cross a stile on the left. Go half-right over a field, with the Dove on the left, and cross a stile at the far end. Climb a bank to follow a path between a hedge and woodland, as far as a Staffordshire Way signpost. Follow this to the left over a stile and bear right along a field edge with woodland on the left. The path eventually swings right to reach a junction of tracks at a signpost.*

3. *Turn right, following the Doveridge bridleway sign. Beyond a cattle grid, turn left through a gate to follow a public footpath sign. Climb a field to a stile to the right of a barn (yellow arrow). At the top of the slope, a trig. point can be seen through the hedge on the left. Climb a stile (yellow arrow) and turn right in front of Upper Eaton Farm to cross a field and reach a metal gate. Follow the line of the yellow arrow down a field, and from the hollow climb to a gate between two hedges. Keep a hedge on the right and pass through another gate to a stile in a fence over a ditch. The path now dips gently, still with a hedge on the right, to pass through a gap and down the middle of a field to a metal gate leading to a road at a bend sign, opposite a white cottage at Waldley.*

4. *Turn left and then right at a junction. 20 metres beyond Waldley Manor (cattle farm), turn right through a metal gate (sign may be missing) and climb a bridleway with a hedge on the left. Cross the fence at the top left-hand corner and keep a hedge on the left to the next corner.*

5. *Turn right here along a hedge for 100 metres to reach a gate. Go through and descend a field to a bridge-stile at the bottom right-hand corner. Climb to the right of a farm to cross a fence-stile in a holly hedge. Turn left, and in 15 metres, right down the farm track to a bridge and a hedge gap. Keep on the same line to reach a*

Continued on page 34

hedge on the left and follow the field margin. In about half a mile, at a sharp right-hand bend, keep straight on, crossing 3 stiles, with Somersal Farm on the right. Descend to Somersal Herbert, reaching the road at a signpost opposite a phone box.

6. *Turn right, passing the Hall and church. Immediately beyond the churchyard, turn left over a stile to follow the Doveridge signpost. The path passes close to oak trees on the right before reaching a stile in a hedge. Cross a long field to a footbridge by a power pole and continue, to cross another field to reach a track by a stile at the top left-hand corner.*

7. *The route passes Field Farm to reach a road. Turn left back to Doveridge, crossing the A50* ***with care*** *by the Cavendish Arms to reach Cook Lane. Church Lane is the third on the right.*

Refreshments
Cavendish Arms, Doveridge.

Bridge over the River Ecclesbourne

Ecclesbourne Valley

Outline

Duffield – Ecclesbourne Valley – Windley Meadows – Windley Hill Farm – Ecclesbourne Valley – Duffield.

Summary

Apart from the short and gentle climb from the B5023 to Windley Hill Farm, this walk is an easy ramble along the valley of the River Ecclesbourne, to the north-west of Duffield. After leaving the village, the route follows public footpaths, with retracing of steps for the last half-mile after a brief encounter with industry in the shape of a colour works, across the yard of which the return route passes. Otherwise the scenery is pleasant if not striking, with the writhings of the little river providing interest throughout.

Attractions

Anyone standing on the bridge in the middle of Duffield could be forgiven for dismissing the stream channelled between concrete walls below as being unworthy of a second glance.

A mile or so westwards, however, this same stream picks its way prettily along a tree-lined valley, a tributary river of the great Derwent, but with a charm and character entirely its own.

And despite its ignominious passage through Duffield to its confluence with the Derwent beyond, the Ecclesbourne boasts one unique distinction – it has the longest name of any English river! In fact the twelve letters of its name exceed the number of miles of its length – a mere eight – from its source near Wirksworth to its meeting with the Derwent at Duffield.

History has seen many changes along this tiny valley. From Norman times until the early 16th century, the hilly country to the north was part of Duffield Frith, a royal hunting forest in which King Edward I pursued the fallow deer. Even as late as 1560, when the forest was already shrinking, it measured 30 miles round and contained over 100,000 oaks. By this time, however, lead and iron smelting were increasing and their greed for fuel hastened the end of the old forest.

Meanwhile industry began to affect the valley itself. Water mills for grinding corn had been established on the Ecclesbourne since Saxon times but by the 19th century, no less than nine mills of various kinds were working along the lower reaches of the little river. The railway too, had arrived by this time and a line was built along the valley up to Wirksworth.

Today, apart from the colour works seen on the closing stages of the walk, the tiny Ecclesbourne has returned to peaceful times. The rails gather rust and sheep graze undisturbed in the riverside pastures. Nature, meanwhile, abounds to enrich

Continued on page 38

Route 7

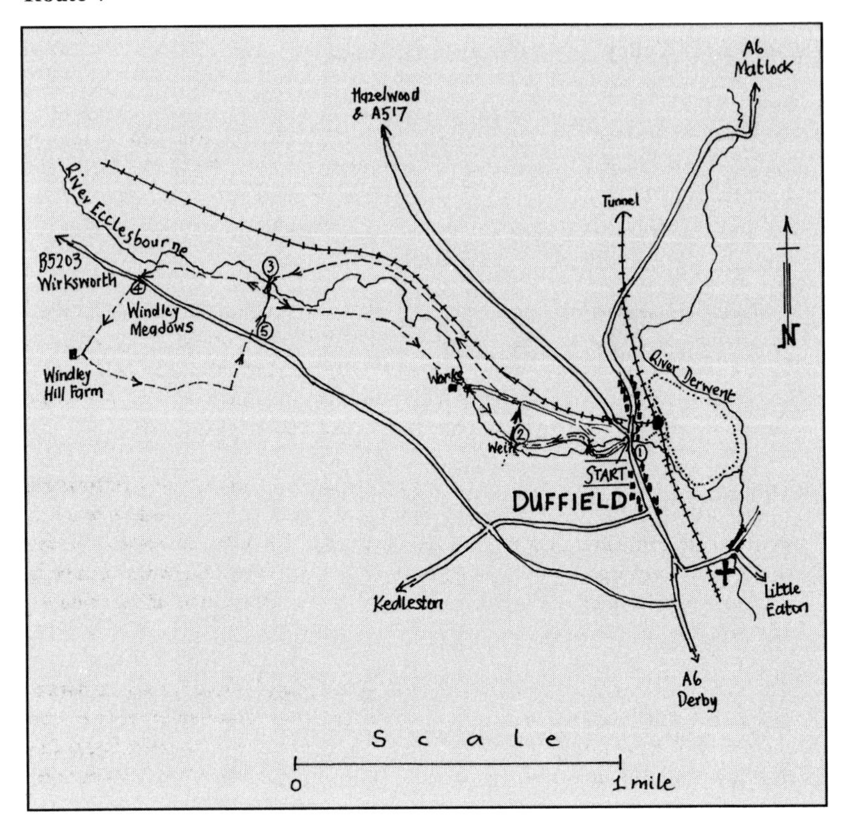
A6
Matlock
Hazelwood
& A517
Tunnel
River Ecclesbourne
B5203
Wirksworth
Windley
Meadows
Windley
Hill Farm
Works
Weir
START
DUFFIELD
River Derwent
N
Kedleston
Little
Eaton
A6
Derby
Scale
0
1 mile

Route 7

Ecclesbourne Valley $4\frac{1}{4}$ miles

Start

Duffield, a village on the A6 between Derby and Belper. The walk starts from the bridge over the River Ecclesbourne on the A6, alongside which is Tamworth Street. Park on the left down this street or elsewhere in the village (OS Landranger Sheet 128. GR 344435).

Route

1. *Walk along Tamworth Street. Cross the Ecclesbourne over another bridge and turn left to join Crown Street. Keep left along this as far as a riverside footpath with a 'No cycling' sign. This path leads to a road with a playground on the right. Keep on as far as a bridge on the left. Do not cross but go through a squeeze stile ahead, passing a weir and following the river as far as another squeeze stile.*

2. *Turn right here and cross 2 stiles to reach a road. Turn left along it and in 50 metres, go right along a signposted footpath between hedges, with a railway line on the right. Cross a stile and keep straight on for about half a mile, after which the path veers left through a gateway to follow the meandering river. Cross a stile in a hedge at a sharp bend and go over a field half-left to a riverside squeeze stile leading to a cart bridge.*

3. *Cross this and turn right to follow the south bank through a squeeze stile and past a gated cart bridge, then swing left along a hedge for 30 metres to cross a stiled footbridge. Cross a large field to a stile and plank bridge and go over one last field to a stile half way along the hedge, giving access to the B5023. Cross with care and turn left for 30 metres to reach a farm track on the right.*

4. *Climb to Windley Hill Farm. Just before reaching the farmhouse, turn left down a narrow field and go through the right-hand of 2 gates. Keep on through another gate to reach a stile in the hedge ahead and continue to reach a track. Turn left along it down to the B5023.*

5. *Cross the busy road once more and follow the public footpath sign over 2 stiles and down to the bridge crossed earlier. This time however, instead of crossing, turn right along the river bank and go over 4 stiles and a large field to enter a colour works yard through a squeeze stile in the wall. Cross the yard and go over a bridge, beyond which is a signpost. Follow the Duffield sign towards a white house to rejoin the outward route near the weir. Retrace to the start.*

the walk. In spring, the bubbling calls of curlews and the cries and wing-beats of peewits fill the air. Skylarks soar above the wide acres of Windley Meadows and there is always the chance of spotting the metallic blue flash of a speeding kingfisher, even close to the bustle of Duffield.

For those who wish to follow the Ecclesbourne to its meeting with the Derwent, a pleasant loop-walk along the well-used water meadows path should set the seal on an enjoyable day.

Refreshments
Pubs and cafes in Duffield. Or what about a riverside picnic?

Shipley Country Park

Route 8 **$3\frac{3}{4}$ miles**

Shipley Country Park

Outline

Information Centre – John Wood – Mapperley Reservoir – Shipley Hill – Osborne's Pond – Information Centre.

Summary

Despite the grimness of its approaches, this extensive country park is a vast oasis in an industrial desert, offering easy access to varied countryside yet retaining much evidence of its chequered past. The walking is easy, with only one gentle climb, and there is scope to extend the route for those equipped with a copy of the simple map on sale at the Information Centre. (Note: The adjacent American Adventure theme park is a separate concern and is not accessible from the Country Park.)

Attractions

Extending over 600 acres, Shipley Country Park is by far the largest open-access area in Derbyshire. It can be explored along footpaths, bridleways and estate roads and comprises woodland, parkland, grazing land, lakes and ponds.

Shipley manor has been in existence for almost 1000 years. It is recorded in the Domesday Book (1086) and was owned by several influential families before it became the property of the Miller Mundys in 1729. Shipley Hall, their family seat, stood on a hilltop commanding wide views. It was described as an elegant stone structure and although it was demolished in 1944, after the Miller Mundys departed, visitors can get some idea of its size by walking round its site and of its appearance by studying the model in the Visitor Centre.

Much of the Miller Mundys' wealth came from their coalmines, as a book written in the 1890s reveals: 'There are two pits in operation, both fitted with the most improved machinery. Almost 1800 men and boys are employed, who turn out about 2000 tons per day.' Ironically, it was the subsidence of the foundations, caused by coal extraction below, that led to the demolition of the hall after the Miller Mundys had sold the estate to the local colliery company.

Although mining ceased in the Shipley area several years ago, traces of the industry can still be seen. They include the headgear of Mapperley Colliery in the adjacent theme park and the old colliery railway line, now a bridleway, and walked on the final stages of the route.

The variety of natural habitat found within the park provides an abundance of wildlife. Both Mapperley Reservoir and Osborne's Pond offer rewarding bird-watching, with mute swans, Canada geese, great-crested grebes, tufted duck, mallard and coot prominent. The woodland areas are well populated with small tree-loving species. These include great, blue and coal tit, nuthatch, treecreeper and great-spotted woodpecker, which in spring reveals its presence by its persistent hammering.

Continued on page 42

Route 8

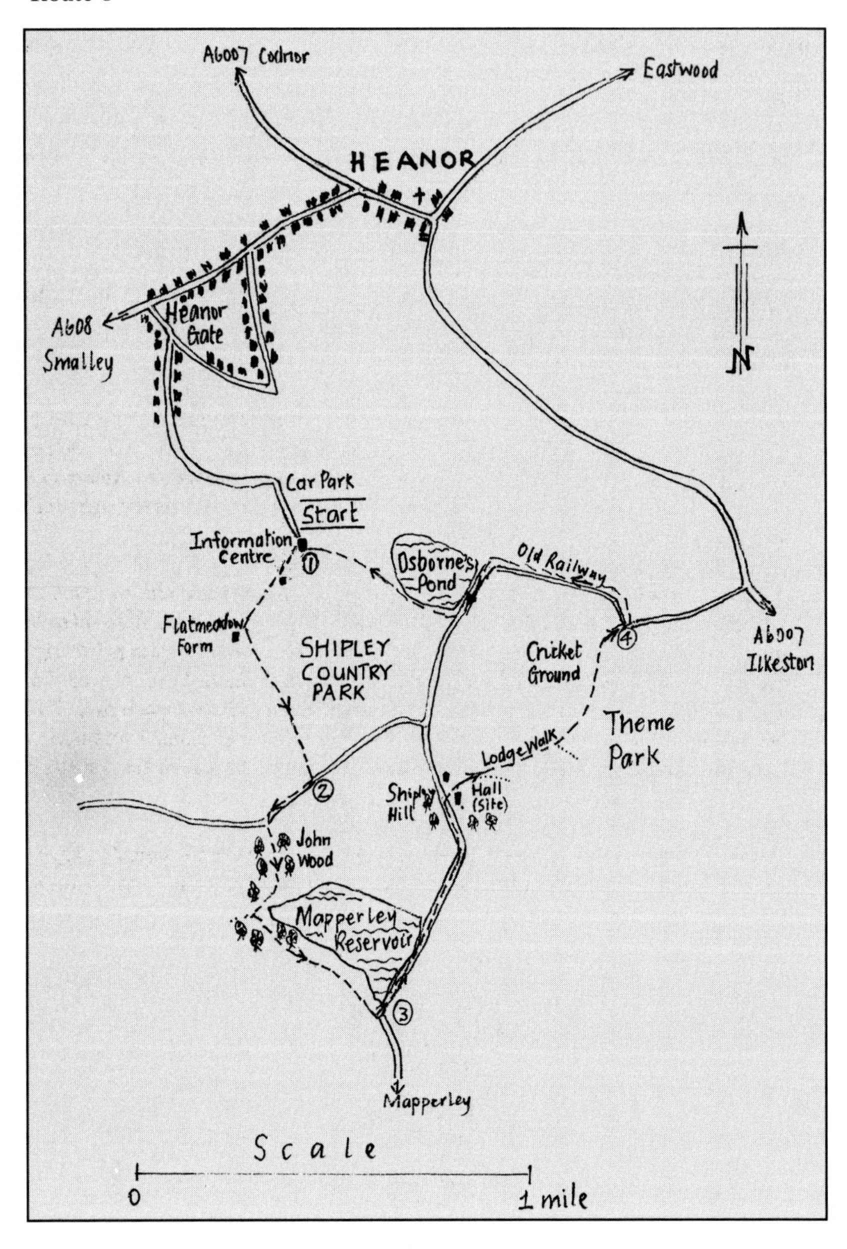
A607 Codnor
Eastwood
HEANOR
Heanor Gate
A608 Smalley
N
Car Park
Start
Information Centre
1
Osborne's Pond
Old Railway
Flatmeadow Farm
SHIPLEY COUNTRY PARK
Cricket Ground
4
A6007 Ilkeston
Theme Park
Lodge Walk
2
Shipley Hill
Hall (Site)
John Wood
Mapperley Reservoir
3
Mapperley
Scale
0
1 mile

Route 8

Shipley Country Park $3\frac{3}{4}$ miles

Start

The Park lies off the A608 at Heanor Gate, south of Heanor town centre. Park in the main car park (OS Landranger Sheet 129. GR 430451). The route begins at the Visitor Centre.

Route

1. *Leave the Visitor Centre through the door on the right, to follow the track to the left from the right-hand extremity of the Park. Pass a private bungalow on the left and continue round a left bend to pass Flatmeadow Farm on the right. Keep a fence on the left as far as a stile by a gate at a T-junction.*

2. *Turn right and continue. Go through a handgate on the left just beyond a bridge over a stream. Enter John Wood, keeping to the right, with a fence on the left, swinging left eventually to reach a fork. Keep left here. Mapperley Reservoir is soon glimpsed on the left through the trees. Keep on, with a fence on the right and a hedge on the left, to reach the reservoir dam.*

3. *Turn left (beware of traffic) to cross the dam. Climb Shipley Hill to reach the turreted building on the summit. Now swing right to go round it and descend to the site of Shipley Hall on the right. From here, follow the drive as it swings left, right and left again down to reach a wall, stretching away to the right. Leave the drive here to follow Lodge Walk, which keeps the wall on the right down to a fork. Take the left-hand route, signposted the Field, along Dog Kennel Lane. The American Adventure theme park can be seen on the right. Pass right of the cricket ground and climb to reach a road.*

4. *Go over and turn left along the bed of the old railway, now a bridleway. Just beyond a bridge, turn left down to Osborne's Pond, beyond which, swing to the right and follow the signs back to the Visitor Centre and the start.*

Wren

Families with energy to spare at the end of the walk can burn it up on the mile-long trim track. Alternatively, cycles can be hired for exploring areas of the park omitted earlier.

Refreshments
Obtainable at the Visitor Centre (Saturdays and Sundays only during winter months). There is a wide choice of picnic places.

The mound on Morley Moor

Route 9 **$4\frac{1}{2}$ miles**

Around Morley

Outline

Morley Lane – Morleymoor – Morley Church – Cloves Wood – Woodside – Brackley Gate – Morley Lane.

Summary

Despite its close proximity to Derby and to a network of busy roads, this absorbing walk follows ancient tracks and well-waymarked footpaths through surprisingly quiet countryside. Apart from the steepish climb from Woodside to the Roman road near Brackley Gate, gradients are gentle and the views, historical interest and wildlife provide constant interest throughout.

Attractions

It would be hard to find a walk offering more attractions for all ages and interests than this, yet surprisingly Morley receives scant attention from some of the guidebooks. In order to avoid omitting any of the notable features likely to appeal to families, these are listed below in the order in which they are encountered along the route.

Almshouses: These were built in 1656 with money left in his will by Jacinth Sacheverall, the lord of the manor. There are 6 houses, 3 intended for each of the poor folk of Morley and its neighbour, Smalley.

The Mound: This is reached along a winding ancient track bordered by old hedges, chiefly of holly, and associated with the Portway, a pre-Roman route. People still argue about the purpose for which the mound was built. Although moated like a castle mound, it is far too small to have served in that capacity and is more likely to have been a lookout or a meeting place of some kind.

St Matthew's Church: This fine Norman church, topped by a splendid 15th century spire, is a treasure house of beautiful architectural features, monuments and stained glass, brought here from Dale Abbey after its destruction in the 16th century. Unfortunately, because of the risk of theft and damage, St Matthew's is open to visitors only on Saturday afternoons (2–4 pm) between April and September. However, there is plenty to see close by, including the mausoleum of the Sitwell family, the former tithe barn, an old cross, and another mound, this time the remains of a tumulus, or prehistoric burial chamber, in the field next to the churchyard.

The water tower: Not just a useful landmark but also a favourite roosting place for tawny owls, the pellets of which litter the floor. Young naturalists may like to take some home and find out what prey the owls have feasted upon.

Continued on page 46

Route 9

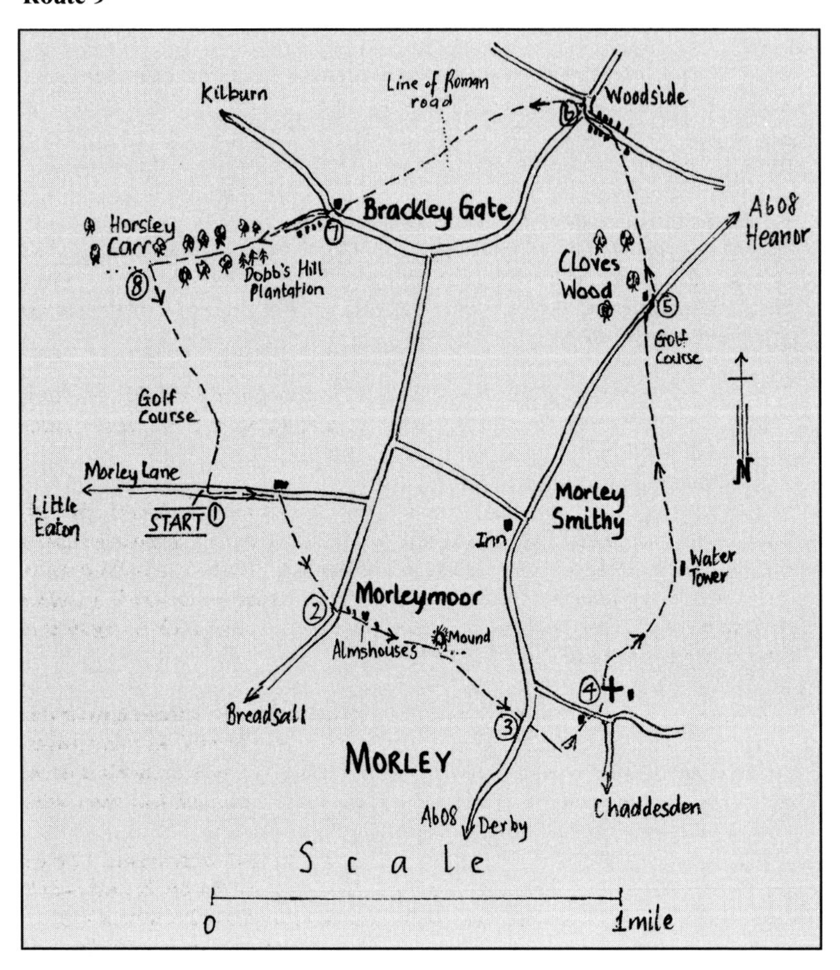

Around Morley **4½ miles**

Start

Morley Lane, an unclassified road linking the B6179 with the A608, and reached either from Little Eaton or from Morley. Park on the verge near the golf course (OS Landranger Sheet 128. GR 381417).

Route 9

Route

1. *Walk along Morley Lane in the direction of Morley, as far as Priory Cottages on the left. Cross a stile opposite and follow the woodland wall to another stile. The route now swings left over scrub before following a fence on the left to reach a road at Morleymoor.*

2. *Cross straight over along Almshouses Lane, passing the almshouses and a chapel. 50 metres beyond, follow a footpath sign on the left. The path follows a hedge on the right to meet a track, which meanders between hedges to reach the Mound. Leave the track here, veering right to cross a footbridge via stiles. Turn left along another track to reach the A608.*

3. *Cross with care and climb the steps. Go over a stile and across a field to another. Cross the next field diagonally left to reach the road past Morley church over a stile at the bottom left-hand corner.*

4. *Climb to the church. Leave the churchyard through the squeeze-stile at the far left-hand corner under a beech tree. Cross a field to the right of a mound and go over a stile in a hedge to reach a track. Turn right, then left at a fork towards a water tower, reached by following a marker post on the left. Leave the tower along a clear path slightly left of the previous line, to reach a stile in a hedge. Cross a golf club drive over stiles to reach the A608.*

5. *Cross and go over a stile by a bungalow. Keep woodland on the left and cross a stile by a power pole. Descend over 3 fields to a stile in a hedge. Beyond, the route crosses another field to reach a road. Turn left down to Woodside and swing right at the Horsley sign. In 40 metres, turn left and follow the public footpath sign over a stile.*

6. *Cross a plank bridge and a stile in a paddock fence and go through a gate. Climb a field to a stile at the top right-hand corner and keep the same line up the next field to another stile. Climb a hillside along the line indicated by the yellow arrow to cross the line of Ryknild Street, from which a stile leads to a stretch of path flanked by a wall on the right. This path skirts Brackley Gate Farm via squeeze stiles to reach a road.*

7. *Turn right and in 50 metres, left along a no-through-road. When the road ends, continue along the track through woodland for about half a mile, as far as a stile on the left, with a public footpath sign.*

8. *Cross this stile and climb through trees to cross a golf course and so reach Morley Lane and the start.*

The Roman road: Between Woodside and Brackley Gate, the route crosses a shallow grassy depression – all that remains of this section of Ryknild Street, the Roman road that linked the Fosse Way at Salmonsbury, near Bourton-on-the-Water in Gloucestershire, with Templeborough, near Rotherham in Yorkshire.

Dobb's Hill plantation: This mixed woodland, together with adjoining Horsley Carr, is rich in bird life. Tits (great, blue and coal) favour this habitat, as do goldcrests and great-spotted woodpeckers. Notice too, the pale corky bracket fungus growing on the birches. This is known as razor strop, as it was once used for sharpening cut-throat razors.

Note

This walk is adapted from one of the excellent country walks leaflets produced by the Erewash Groundwork Trust. Details from the Trust at 43, Town Street, Sandiacre, Nottingham NG10 5DU.

Refreshments

Three Horse Shoes Inn, Morley Smithy (just off route).

Green woodpecker

Route 10 **5 miles**

Dale Abbey and Locko Park

Outline

Dale Abbey – Hermit's Cave (diversion) – Dunnshill – Locko Park lake – Hollies Farm – A6096 (The Flourish) – Dale Abbey.

Summary

This walk, along footpaths and bridleways for its entire length, passes through pleasant, gently undulating country mercifully spared the industrialisation that has blighted so much of the Nottinghamshire–Derbyshire borderland. Be prepared for muddy conditions underfoot, especially between Dale Abbey and Columbine Farm.

Attractions

Southwards from Heanor to the A52 between Ockbrook and Risley lies an all-too-narrow corridor of comparatively unspoilt country, of which the area centred on Dale Abbey is arguably the most attractive. Dale lost its 12th century abbey at the dissolution of the monasteries but the huge surviving arch of the east window can be visited near the start of the walk.

For those in search of the spectacular, however, the tiny church of All Saints is an even greater attraction. Described by a leading authority as 'one of the smallest and oddest of English churches', its interior has changed little with the passing of centuries and it must be unique in being attached to a farmhouse, once an inn!

But to many, especially children, the hermit's cave is Dale's most fascinating feature and the short diversion to see it will be more likely to appeal if they are familiar with the legend relating how it came to be hewn out of the sandstone cliffs.

The story goes that during the reign of Henry I, before the building of the abbey, a Derby baker named Cornelius was taking an afternoon nap when the Virgin Mary appeared to him in a dream and directed him to go to Deepdale and live a life of prayer and solitude there. Cornelius did as he was told and in time excavated a shelter for himself in the barren rocky place. One day, when out hunting, the owner of the land, a knight called Ralph Fitz Geremund, noticed smoke rising from the hermit's fire and rode over to order off the ragged intruder. On hearing the hermit's story, however, he was moved to compassion and not only agreed to allow the hermit to remain but also provided for his maintenance and bestowed on him the tithe money from nearby Borrowash mill.

With this generous help, Cornelius was able to build himself a bigger and more suitable place in which to live and worship and tradition tells us that it was on the site of this building that the present All Saints church now stands.

The greater part of the route between (5) and (6) is along a bridleway between interesting old hedges. Hollies Farm is well named, for these hedges abound with holly bushes.

Route 10

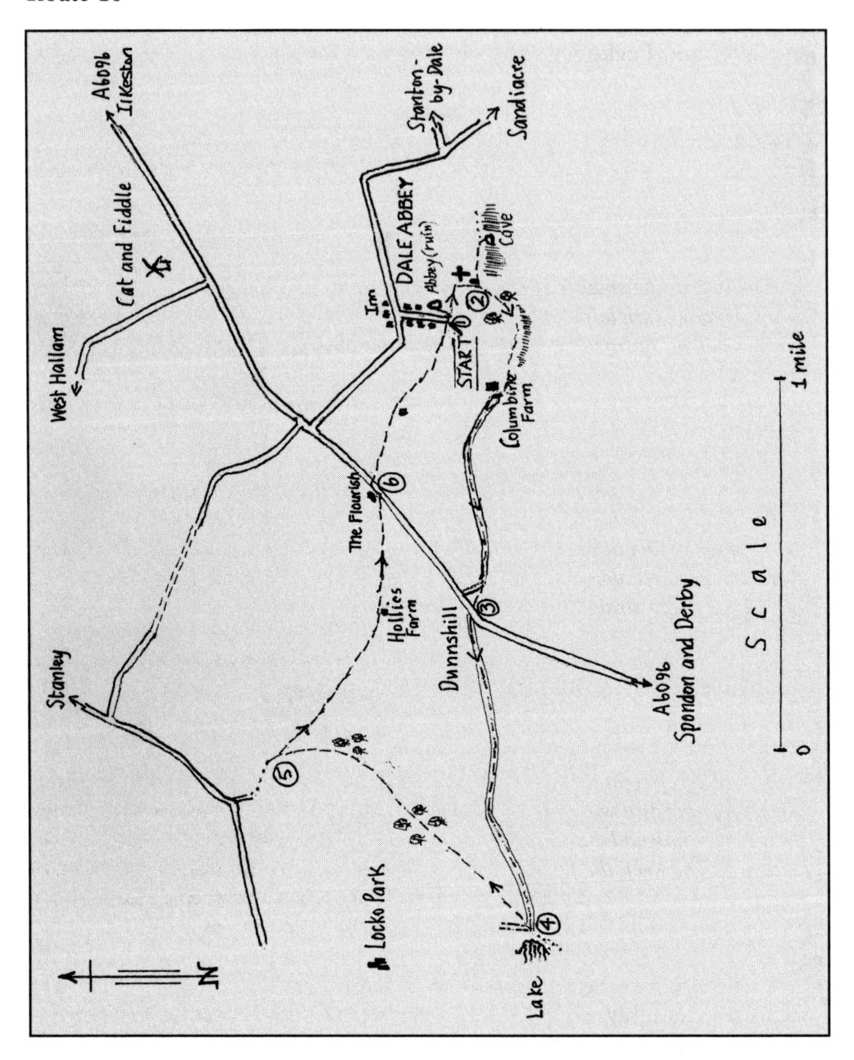
West Hallam
Cat and Fiddle
A6096
Ilkeston
Stanton-by-Dale
Sandiacre
DALE ABBEY
Abbey (ruin)
Inn
Cave
START
Columbine Farm
The Flourish
Hollies Farm
Dunnshill
A6096
Spondon and Derby
Stanley
Locko Park
Lake
N
Scale
0
1 mile

Route 10

Dale Abbey and Locko Park — 5 miles

Start

Dale Abbey, a village ¾ mile south of the A6096, midway between Spondon and Kirk Hallam. Park down the road opposite the Carpenter's Arms (OS Sheet 129. GR 436388).

Route

1. *Walk down to the small green and turn left past the Manor House. (To see the abbey window, turn left and left again over stiles by a white cottage at a bend and walk up a field. Retrace steps.) Pass All Saints church and climb to a handgate on the right opposite a farmhouse and signposted 'Public Bridleway–Dunnshill'. (To see the Hermit's Cave, keep on through the farmyard and follow signs along the clear path. Retrace steps.)*

2. *Climb up to a gate and continue up a track to enter woodland through another gate. Follow the track through the wood and leave by a metal gate. Keep a hedge on the right along the foot of sloping ground to a stile by a gate. Go down past Columbine Farm and turn left along the farm lane, following it until it swings right just before the A6096. Keep straight on here to reach the road.*

3. *Cross with care and continue along the bridleway to Locko Park. Go through a gate and keep right at a fork by a house. Continue as far as a T-junction, with the end of a lake visible ahead.*

4. *Here, turn sharp right through a kissing-gate and follow a public footpath sign over parkland towards a wood. Enter over a ladder-stile (Locko House visible to the left). Leave the wood through a kissing-gate and follow a fence on the right. Cross a footbridge and keep the same line up a fence-side. Pass a stile into a wood on the right and follow the hedge to another stile at the field corner. Keep a hedge on the left as far as a farm road.*

5. *Turn left through a gateway and immediately sharp right through a metal handgate. Keep a hedge on the right to reach another handgate in the field corner. Continue, still with a hedge on the right, swinging left after 2 fields to follow a wide grassy track between the hedge and trees. Keep on through a handgate and, at the top of a slope, bear left towards Hollies Farm (blue arrow). Follow the bridleway as it keeps the farm on the right, to reach The Flourish on the A6096, along the farm road.*

6. *Turn left along the verge for 100 metres before crossing with care to follow a public*

Continued on page 50

footpath sign through a gate. Cross a field by a track leading to a gate and then keep a hedge on the left down to a stile, with a farm below to the right. Keep straight on across a sloping field to a stile at the far corner. Follow a path along a bank as far as a stile in the hedge on the right. Descend to reach a lane, turn left, and continue to the green at Dale Abbey and the start.

Nearby attractions

Cat and Fiddle windmill (1 mile N of Dale, off A6096). Fine example of rare post-mill in good order. Morley church (4 miles NW of Dale). Contains much stained glass from the demolished abbey.

Refreshments

The Carpenter's Arms, Dale Abbey.

Dale Abbey Church

Route 11 **$2\frac{3}{4}$ miles**

Elvaston Castle Country Park

Outline

Official car park – Bedford Drive – Lake Bridge – Elvaston footpath – Golden Gates – The Castle – The Lake – Car park.

Summary

An easy walk, level throughout, along clear, well-surfaced paths. This walk is intended merely as an introduction to this suberb country park, which considering its close proximity to Derby and its popularity generally, retains much of its rural charm. Offering as it does such a range of attractions – parkland, woods, lake, grottoes, gardens, architecture, history, wildlife, children's playground – this is a perfect location for a family outing.

Attractions

A guidebook of some 20 years ago described Elvaston as a secret oasis, bounded on three sides by suburban growth. Now, however, this remarkable 200-acre oasis, the private domain of the Stanhopes (later Earls of Harrington) for four centuries, can be enjoyed by all.

The castle around which the park was laid out dates from the early 19th century, although the brick-built eastern wing is a remnant of an earlier building and bears the date 1633.

Scattered around the grounds are other intriguing buildings, including a Moorish temple and Springthorpe Cottage, passed on the walk, both built with curved walls and looking somewhat bizarre in an otherwise traditional English setting. Close by, too, is St Bartholomew's church, parts of which are of 13th century origin, and which contains some impressive monuments to the Harringtons.

But it is to the spacious and spectacular grounds that most families will be drawn and the delights they offer cannot possibly be covered adequately in this short space. The margins of the ornamental lake, in particular, are irresistible, for here are stony grottoes, rock archways, delightful views of the lake, and plenty of scope for natural history, especially bird-watching.

In fact the Park's bird life features prominently in the excellent nature trail booklet obtainable at the gift shop. It contains helpful drawings and text describing some of the waterfowl likely to be spotted on the lake, including tufted duck, pochard and wigeon, as well as such small woodland species as goldcrest, coal tit and nuthatch.

Observant children will relish a game of 'Spot the nestbox' during the course of the walk. These artificial nesting sites range in size from small enclosed boxes with entrance holes suitable for members of the tit tribe, to large open-ended boxes set at an angle from the trunks of certain trees and intended for use by tawny owls.

Continued on page 54

Route 11

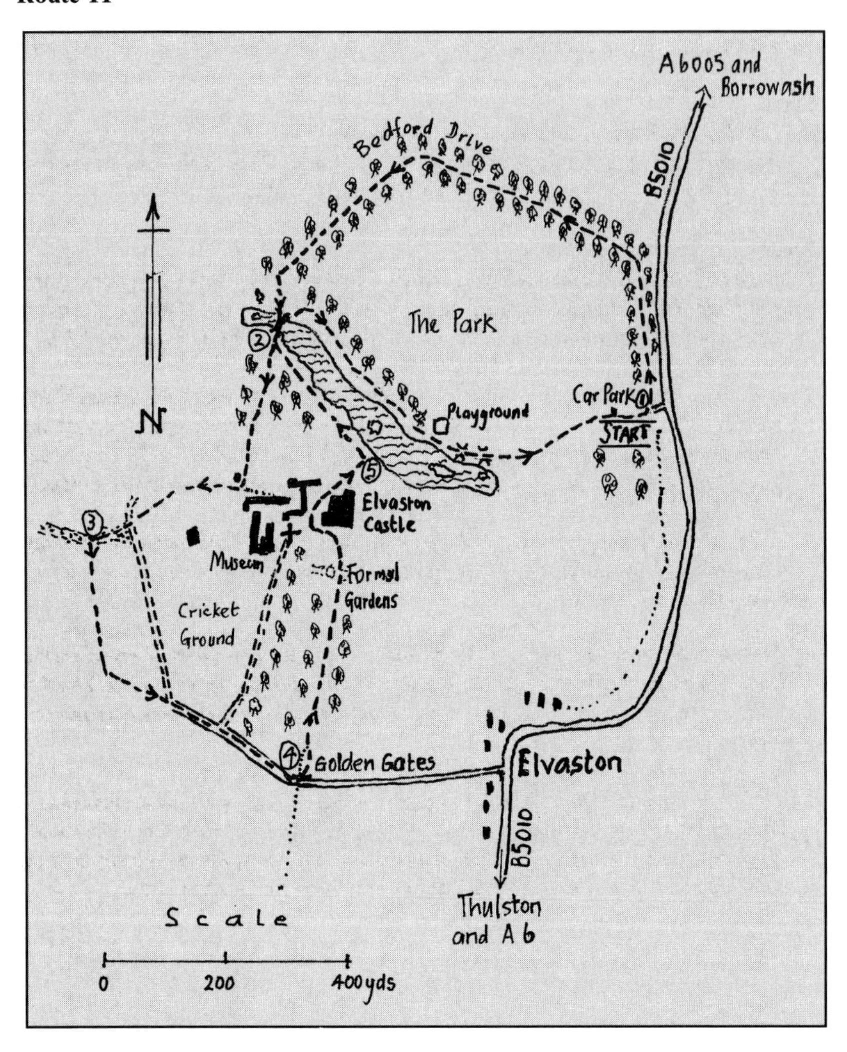
A6005 and
Borrowash
B5010
Bedford Drive
The Park
2
Playground
Car Park 1
START
5
Elvaston
Castle
3
Museum
Formal
Gardens
Cricket
Ground
4
Golden Gates
Elvaston
B5010
Thulston
and A6
Scale
0
200
400 yds

Route 11

Elvaston Castle Country Park $2\frac{3}{4}$ miles

Start

The Country Park lies to the north of Elvaston village, on the B5010, $1\frac{1}{2}$ miles north of its junction with the A6 and 3 miles SE of Derby. Park in the official car park (parking fee) (OS Landranger Sheet 129. GR 412332).

Route

1. *From the car park, walk back towards the B5010 and turn left along the surfaced tree-lined Bedford Drive, just before and parallel to the road. Continue along this drive, ignoring the many tempting side turns, to reach a bridge over the lake.*

2. *Keep on to reach a T-junction of routes, with Elvaston castle and church on the left. Turn right between ornamental gateposts (noticing Springthorpe Cottage) and walk along the raised plankway to reach a crossroads of tracks. The route veers right here and continues to reach a footpath sign on the left indicating Elvaston.*

3. *Follow this path as far as another T-junction. Now turn left again and on reaching a metalled drive, continue along it, passing the entrance to the church, to reach the blue-painted Golden Gates.*

4. *Turn left through the gates, entering the gardens along a formal avenue which leads, via a topiary archway, to the Castle. Go through an archway on the left of the front of the castle and cross a courtyard to the right to reach the lake over terraced lawns.*

5. *Turn left along the lakeside to re-cross the bridge at (2). Turn right immediately beyond and follow the walk, with the lake on the right and rock formations and a children's playground on the left. The car park and the start are reached by crossing two bridges, the second of which leads directly into the parking area.*

Even easier to spot are the dreys of grey squirrels – untidy bunches of twigs and dead leaves wedged into the forks of upper branches of trees along the route.

Finally, the so-called Golden Gates (4) are well worth examining in some detail. They were brought to Elvaston in 1819 from Versailles, where they had been taken by Napoleon Bonaparte from Spain and have been painted blue since about 1850.

More about the Park

As well as the nature trail booklet, the gift shop stocks 4 excellent trail guides, each offering a ½-hour walk. The titles are: *Lakeside Trail, Golden Gates Trail, Gardens Trail, Castle Trail.*

Those wishing to find out more about the history of the castle and its park are recommended to buy the beautifully produced full-colour guidebook which is also available at the gift shop.

Refreshments

Parlour tearooms: morning coffee, light lunches, afternoon teas. Open daily, Easter to end October – 11 am–4.30 pm. Closed Mondays in Spring and Autumn (except Bank Holidays).

Elvaston castle

Route 12 **$2\frac{3}{4}$ miles**

Shardlow – an inland port

Outline

Shardlow – Cavendish Bridge – Long Horse Bridge – Trent and Mersey Canal – Shardlow.

Summary

A short walk, level throughout, chiefly along riverbank and canal towpath, though including a short unavoidable stretch of pavement-walking alongside the A6. The walk is centred on Shardlow, an insignificant little place until the coming of the Trent and Mersey Canal, which transformed the village into an important inland port. Many traces of its former prosperity can be seen on this easy yet absorbing walk.

Attractions

It was in 1766 that work started at Shardlow to construct a 93-mile-long canal to link the rivers Trent and Mersey, at that time a most daring and revolutionary feat. In charge was Derbyshire-born James Brindley, a self-taught millwright and civil engineer, who saw what he called 'water roads' as the ideal means of improving the country's primitive transport system, which was based on a combination of poorly-maintained roads and unsuitable rivers.

The 'Canal Age' came and went long ago, leaving some inland waterways to decay and others, like the Trent and Mersey Canal, to survive for recreational use by narrow-boat enthusiasts and pleasure-boaters. Fortunately, much of the inland transhipment port of Shardlow, too, has survived, and is now scheduled as a conservation area. A canal-towpath walk reveals massive warehouses and wharves where such goods as coal, iron, lead, salt, cotton, pottery, cheese, ale and malt were stored and loaded, where cranes swung busily overhead, and where skilled craftsmen of many kinds – boat-builders and repairers, smiths, rope-makers and chandlers – all plied their trades.

The names of the inns – the Navigation, the Ship, the Canal Tavern – all serve as reminders of past prosperity, while the iron mileposts, indicating the distance to the northern end of the canal at Preston Brook, near Runcorn, are further proof of Shardlow's importance as the southern limit of one of the country's most important inland waterways. However, this does not mean that Shardlow is merely a 'ghost port'. There are still plenty of boats to see, ranging from converted traditional narrow boats, with their brightly-painted livery and ports of origin proudly displayed, to pleasure craft of every imaginable kind at the marina.

The walk crosses two interesting bridges. The first, Cavendish Bridge, spanning the Trent and linking Derbyshire with Leicestershire, replaced the original bridge in 1960. By its side stands the old tollboard, with its fascinating list of charges, ranging

Continued on page 58

Route 12

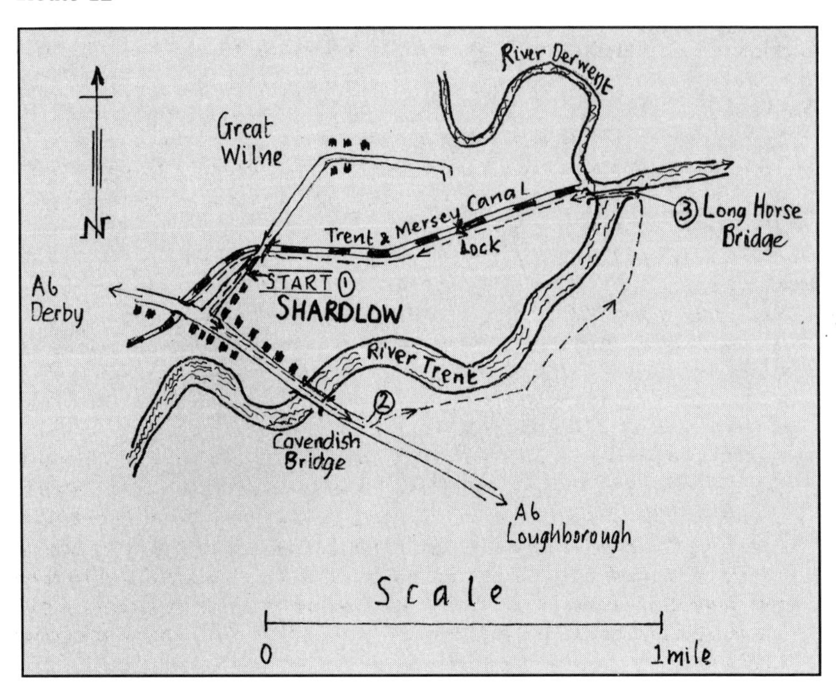

Canada geese

Route 12

Shardlow – an inland port $2\frac{3}{4}$ miles

Start

Wilne Lane car park, Shardlow. Shardlow lies on the A6, 7 miles SE of Derby. The car park is reached by following the signpost 'Great Wilne only' on the left, a short distance before reaching Cavendish Bridge (OS Landranger Sheet 129. GR 445304).

Route

1. *Walk back along Wilne Lane to its junction with the A6. Turn left along the pavement by the Navigation Inn and continue along the pavement/verge over Cavendish Bridge. (Tolls notice on the right just before the bridge.) Beyond the bridge, take the first turn on the left.*

2. *Follow the public footpath sign over a stile and across a long field, keeping as near as possible in the direction of the signpost arrow, to reach the bank of the River Trent. Turn right and follow the river for about $\frac{3}{4}$ mile, as far as Long Horse Bridge, a footbridge over the Trent near its meeting place with its tributary, the Derwent. This riverside walk can be somewhat overgrown in places but yellow arrows on posts indicate the easiest route. However, be sure to ignore one such arrow, which marks the direction of another path, leading away from the river towards gravel diggings.*

3. *Cross Long Horse Bridge and continue for about a mile along the towpath of the Trent and Mersey Canal, passing Derwent Mouth Lock, back to Shardlow. The car park can be reached from the first bridge by passing under, climbing to the road, and turning right. Alternatively, those wishing to see more of the canal, its boats and associated buildings, can continue as far as the A6 bridge and return to the car park from here.*

from two shillings and sixpence for coaches to a halfpenny for soldiers. The second bridge, a footbridge known as Long Horse Bridge, re-crosses the Trent opposite the mouth of the River Derwent, here completing its 60-mile journey from the slopes of Bleaklow in the Dark Peak, through Matlock and Derby.

Nearby, on the way back to Shardlow, is a chance to watch boats negotiating Derwent Mouth Lock, a procedure likely to appeal to all members of the family.

Refreshments
Choice of inns at Shardlow.

Swarkestone Junction

Barrow-upon-Trent and Swarkestone

Outline

Barrow-upon-Trent – Swarkestone Bridge – Swarkestone Church – Summer House (optional) – Trent and Mersey Canal – Barrow-upon-Trent.

Summary

Virtually flat throughout, this Trent Valley walk follows fieldpaths, minor roads and a canal towpath, although care should be taken in the crossing of 3 busy roads. There is plenty of historical and wildlife interest along the route and although the bustling world of traffic and industry is never far away, much remains of less strident times to provide relaxation, interest and a sense of achievement.

Attractions

Near neighbours on the north bank of the River Trent, Barrow and Swarkestone have fared very differently with the passing of the centuries. Sandwiched between the busy A5132 and the river, Barrow is a sleepy backwater. All that remains of its burnt-out mansion is a quaint little lodge in the centre of the village and most of its notable features, including the church and the former pinfold (enclosure for stray cattle) almost opposite, are strung out along a quiet lane that peters out to end in the riverside walk to Swarkestone along which the walk passes.

Swarkestone, by contrast, boasts a colourful history. It stands at the meeting of two busy roads and its famous bridge and $\frac{3}{4}$-mile causeway are believed to date from the 13th century when, according to legend, they were built by two sisters in memory of the young men to whom they were betrothed and who had been drowned attempting to cross the river.

This remarkable bridge has its own special place in our national history. In 1745, the Scottish army, led by Bonnie Prince Charlie, the Young Pretender, reached this river-crossing on their march south, before abandoning their plans to advance on London.

A century or so earlier, Swarkestone Hall, the home of the Royalist Sir John Harpur, had been demolished on the orders of Cromwell's parliament. The present hall, which can be seen on the right from the diversion from the church, was built from some of the remains, while the twin-towered summer house nearby may have been used as a grandstand for watching jousting and bull-baiting.

As with Route 12, this walk includes a stretch of the towpath of the Trent and Mersey Canal, the 93-mile-long waterway linking the Trent at Shardlow with the Mersey at Preston Brook, near Runcorn. The canal is the work of the Derbyshire-born waterways pioneer James Brindley. Swarkestone Lock provides the opportunity to see how canal builders managed to build their waterways so as to minimise water-loss on gradients. Brindley avoided locks whenever he could by taking his

Continued on page 62

Route 13

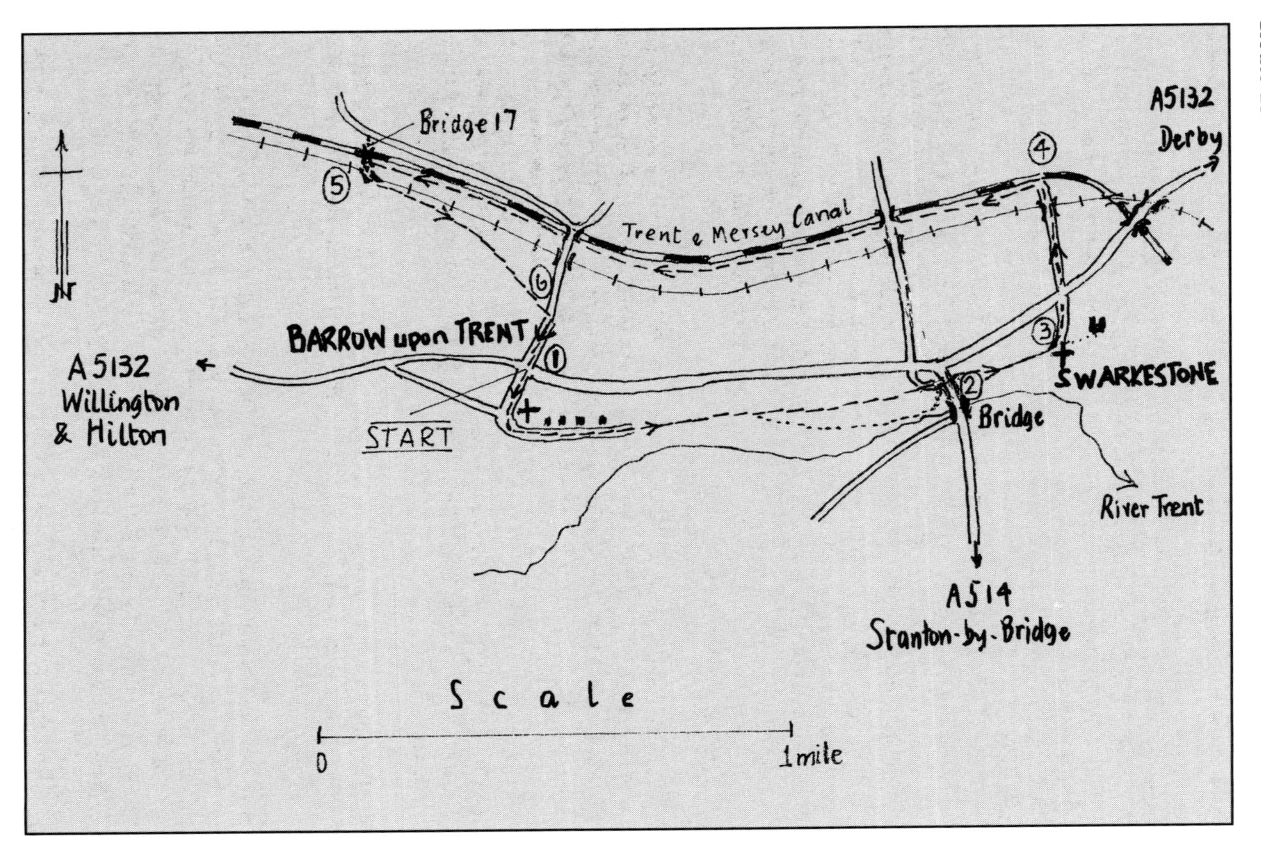
A5132
Derby
Bridge 17
Trent & Mersey Canal
BARROW upon TRENT
A5132
Willington
& Hilton
START
SWARKESTONE
Bridge
River Trent
A514
Stanton-by-Bridge
N
1
2
3
4
5
6
S c a l e
0
1 mile

Route 13

Barrow-upon-Trent and Swarkestone — $4\frac{1}{2}$ miles

Start

Barrow-upon-Trent, a village off the A5132, 2 miles west of its junction with the A514 at Swarkestone. Park in the village (OS Landranger Sheet 128. GR 354285).

Route

1. *Walk along Church Lane, a no-through-road. Follow this, swinging to the left past the church and several houses and farms, to its end. Here, continue along a riverside footpath (yellow arrow). Cross a footbridge and keep straight on. At the end of the first field, the public right-of-way leaves the well-used riverbank path and strikes off diagonally left over a large arable field, passing a wood on the left. Continue through a gap in a fence and cross 2 small fields to reach a stile by Meadow Farm. However, as this footpath is little used, families may prefer to continue along the riverside path, which, after crossing a stile, links up with the other path just before the farm. Immediately beyond the farm, the route reaches a minor road (Woodshop Lane) at Swarkestone.*

2. *Turn right and cross the A514 with great care. Follow the public footpath sign (i.e. along the left of 2 paths), crossing stiles and continuing to reach a lane opposite Swarkestone church. To see the Summer House, go through the churchyard and leave over 2 stiles on the left. The path swings right along the field edge to reach a track. The twin towers can be seen ahead on the left. Retrace your steps.*

3. *Turn left along Church Lane and follow it to its junction with the A5132. Cross with care and walk along Pingle Lane to reach the towpath of the Trent and Mersey Canal.*

4. *Turn left along the towpath and follow it for about $1\frac{1}{2}$ miles, passing Swarkestone Lock and the junction of the old Derby Canal. Continue as far as Bridge 17 (Deep Dale Bridge).*

5. *Leave the towpath here and turn left along a track. 15 metres beyond a railway bridge, cross a stile on the left (yellow arrow) and descend the bank (difficult after rain) to cross a plank bridge and another stile. Keep a hedge on the left over a field to a third stile. The route now strikes half-right over another field to a bridge-stile, beyond which it keeps a hedge on the left as far as the next stile. From this point, the path leads to a road, reached over a stile by a gate.*

6. *Turn right to reach the A5132. Cross with care and carry straight on down Brookfield into Barrow and the start.*

canals in sweeping curves but this is an early example of his use of the lock, still operating efficiently after over 200 years' service.

Nearby is the junction of an abandoned waterway, the old Derby Canal, now derelict and forgotten, except by a few canal enthusiasts.

Refreshments
The Crewe and Harpur Arms, Swarkestone.

The Summer House, Swarkestone

Route 14 **$4\frac{1}{4}$ miles**

Ingleby and Foremark

Outline

Ingleby – Anchor Church – Foremark Church (diversion – optional) – Foremark – Seven Spouts Farm – Ingleby.

Summary

This walk, along quiet footpaths and bridleways, ends with a short road section through the Trent-side village of Ingleby. The few gradients encountered are gentle, although after prolonged rain it may be necessary to take a short but somewhat precipitous detour over part of the riverside cliff to reach Anchor Church (not recommended for young children). History and wildlife interest provide plenty of stimulus throughout.

Attractions

Nowhere on its journey through South Derbyshire is the Trent more beautiful than at Ingleby. Sweeping round a sharp bend from the west, the river steadies its course and flows by a range of sandstone cliffs, along which the walk from Ingleby village begins.

The clifftop views are some of the best along the entire Trent valley, and even on misty days, it is still possible to watch gulls and cormorants beating their way low along the water. Gorse grows in profusion along the route and its yellow bloom splashes welcome brightness even on grey colourless days.

Anchor Church is not a place of worship but a large cave divided into small chambers. It is said to have been the home of a hermit, although in later times it was used by Sir Francis Burdett, of Foremark Hall, as a picnic place and fishing temple. Notice the bricks built into the rock walls where a door was fitted. A little further on along the walk is a smaller cave, with a 'built-in' cupboard, known locally as 'The Anchorite's Larder'.

Although just off the route, St Saviour's church, Foremark, is well worth the short diversion. It was one of the first English churches to be built after the restoration of the monarchy and dates from 1662. Few small churches offer so much to see – a three-decker canopied pulpit, box pews, massive exposed oak beams (brought from the demolished church at Ingleby) and a fascinating collection of monuments, including several to members of the Burdett family, former owners of the nearby hall.

An excellent history of Foremark and district is on sale in the church. It contains a tribute to the social reformer Sir Francis Burdett and also the gory Legend of the Severed Hand – a local ghost story guaranteed to bury even the most reluctant young reader's nose in the book!

Foremark Hall, built for Sir Robert Burdett in 1755, has for some years served as the preparatory school for Repton, the nearby public school.

Continued on page 66

Route 14

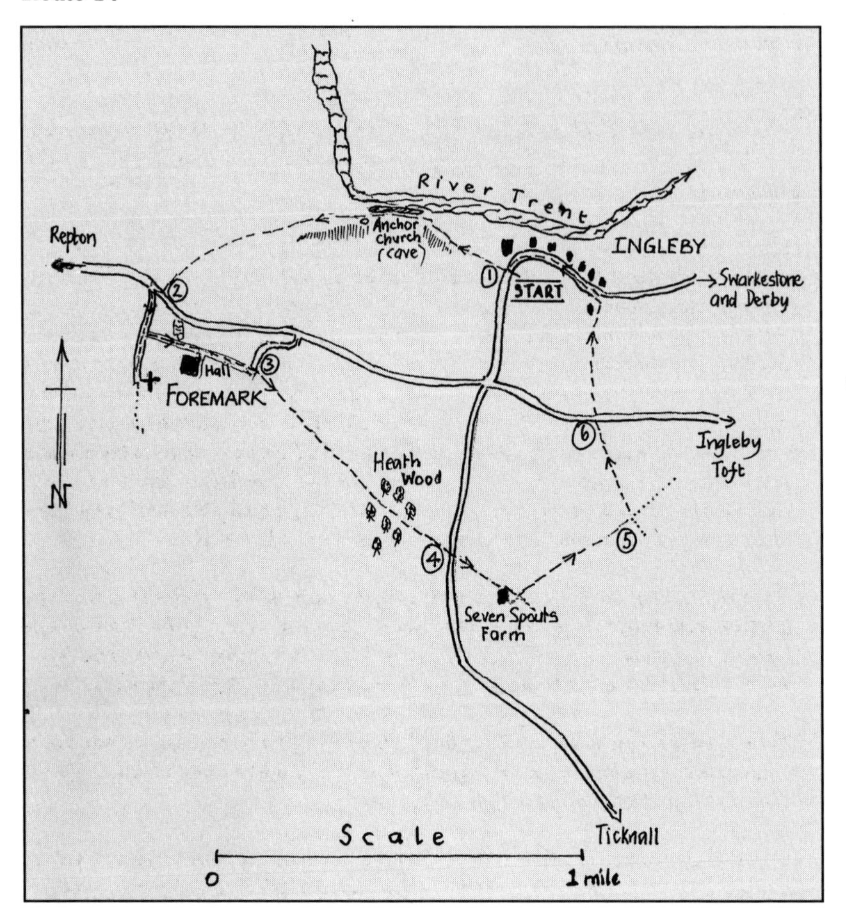

River Trent
Anchor Church (cave)
INGLEBY
START
Repton
Swarkestone and Derby
Hall
FOREMARK
Heath Wood
Ingleby Toft
Seven Spouts Farm
Ticknall
N
1
2
3
4
5
6
Scale
0
1 mile

Route 14

Ingleby and Foremark — $4\frac{1}{4}$ miles

Start

Ingleby, a village 2 miles SW of the A5132–A514 junction at Swarkestone Bridge. Park on a wide stretch of verge just beyond the west end of the village (OS Landranger Sheet 128. GR 347270).

Route

1. *Cross the road and follow the public bridleway sign through a metal gate. Climb a field edge to a second gate and keep on the same line to reach a stile above the River Trent. The clear path follows the river, dipping eventually to cross a stile at river level. Ignore a cart bridge on the right and keep straight on, with a cliff face above to the left, to reach Anchor Church. (Note: After prolonged wet weather, it may be necessary to climb over the first section of cliff by a steep path to reach Anchor Church – a difficult climb unsuitable for young children.) Beyond Anchor Church, cross a fence at a gap in the cliffs and continue on the same line to meet a track, with a conifer plantation on the right. Cross a stile by a gate and follow the track as it climbs by a beech avenue before swinging left to reach a road.*

2. *Turn right along the road for 20 metres before turning left up Home Farm drive. The route turns left along the private road to Foremark Hall, a public right of way. (To see St Saviour's church, keep on up the drive.) Resuming the route, pass left of Foremark Hall and continue along the main drive to reach a phone box.*

3. *Follow the track to the right of the phone box. Proceed along an avenue and cross a stile to enter woodland. (Viking grave mounds visible under trees.) Leave the wood over a stile and keep on to meet a road.*

4. *Cross straight over. The route dips to Seven Springs Farm. Take the left-hand of 3 alternatives – a track with woodland on the right. After passing left of a pond, the track dips gently to meet a cross-track.*

5. *Turn left through a gateway and climb a slope. Pass under power lines and continue through a hedge gap. Beyond, keep a hedge on the left as far as a minor road.*

6. *Cross straight over and go through a gate, following the hedge on the right to pass through a wooden gate in the hedge about 50 metres before the field corner. The route concludes along a sunken lane, passing a house on the left and descending to Ingleby. Turn left along the road back to the start.*

On either side of the track through Heath Wood, between Foremark and Seven Spouts Farm, can be seen a series of ridged mounds. These mark the site of a Danish cemetery, in which the cremated remains of some 60 Viking settlers were buried during the late 9th century. Archaeological excavations some years ago yielded fragments of bones, swords, buckles and other remains.

Refreshments
There are pubs at Milton and Repton close by. Alternatively, the Orange Hill viewpoint overlooking Foremark Reservoir (2 miles south) is ideal for a picnic.

Anchor Church, Ingleby

Route 15 **$3\frac{1}{4}$ miles**

Bretby Village and Park

Outline

Bretby Village – Hartshorne Road – Bretby Park – Bretby Hall – Bretby Village.

Summary

A walk of gentle climbs and descents, chiefly along footpaths and tracks through sheep pasture, woods and parkland. Care is needed along the second short stretch of road walking. This short walk is rich both in wildlife potential and historical associations.

Attractions

Bretby is a tiny village today but this was not always so. Its population in 1891 was 377. It had a colliery then, providing work for many of the menfolk, the others being employed chiefly on the Hall estate, as butlers, coachmen, grooms, gardeners and gamekeepers, while their wives and daughters carried out such duties as cook, housekeeper, maid, dairymaid, and so on.

In the vicinity of the little village green can be seen several reminders of Bretby's busier past. The war memorial, in the unusual form of a pump shelter, bears the names of the thirteen local men who died in the First World War, while on the right stands the former village school, opened, as the plaque reveals, in 1806. It was built by the Earl of Chesterfield to accommodate 24 boys and the same number of girls.

In the nearby church, rebuilt in 1878, is a brass tablet to the Victorian prime minister, Benjamin Disraeli, later Lord Beaconsfield, who often stayed at Bretby Hall. He is described as 'the foremost man of his age'. On private ground to the south-west of the church are a number of mounds – all that remains of Bretby Castle, which dominated the village for almost 300 years until its demolition in 1610.

Bretby Hall, which has been a hospital since 1926, is the second great house to stand here. It was built for the 5th Earl of Chesterfield in 1813–15 by the architect Sir Jeffry Wyattville, famous for his work on Chatsworth House.

The walk gives impressive views of the Hall and of part of the extensive grounds, especially the ornamental lakes. These attract a good variety of water birds, the most striking of which is the great-crested grebe, a graceful white-necked bird which often dives under water for its food. The more open expanses of the park provide suitable habitat for the little owl, a bird introduced into this country about 150 years ago. It became well-established here early in the present century before spreading throughout south Derbyshire.

Although the first Bretby Hall was pulled down in 1780, we can read a description of it, written by an early travel writer, Celia Fiennes, after her visit in

Continued on page 70

Route 15

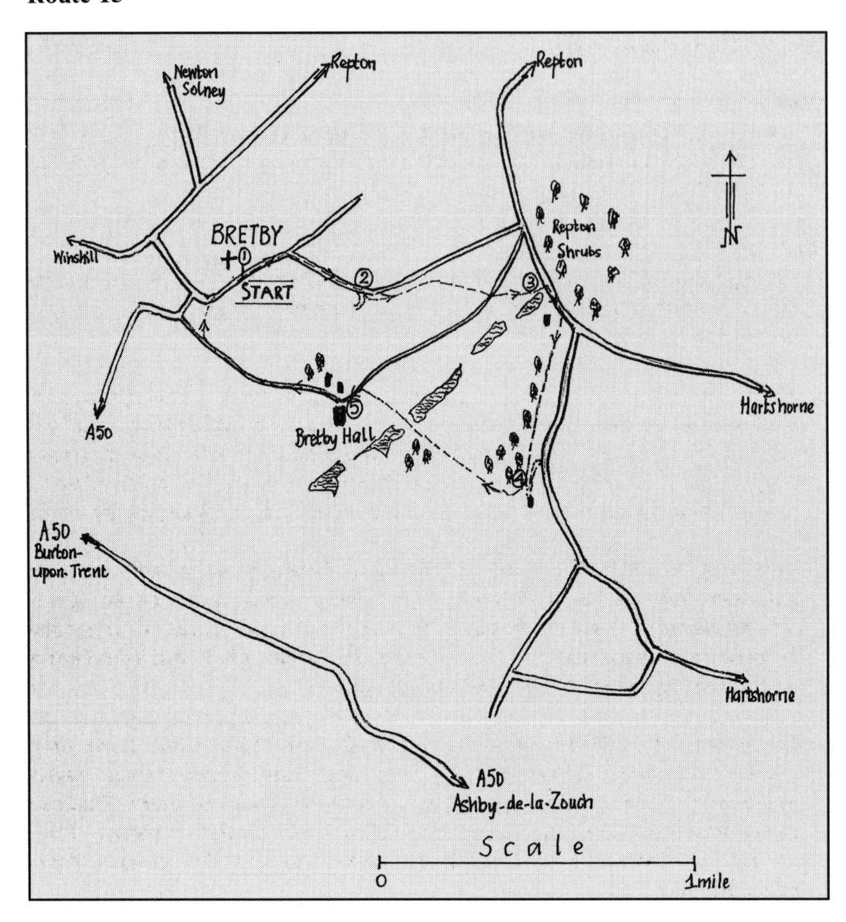

Little owl

Route 15

Bretby Village and Park — $3\frac{1}{4}$ miles

Start

Bretby, a village $1\frac{1}{2}$ miles north of the A50 and 4 miles east of Burton-upon-Trent. Park as near as possible to the triangular village green (O.S. Landranger Sheet 128. GR 295232).

Route

1. *Facing the road from the green, turn left along it. Swing right at the Hartshorne signpost. In about half a mile, watch for a private road on the right between two areas of woodland.*

2. *Follow this road for 30 metres and go through a gate on the left, leading to a public bridleway through woodland. Leave the wood through a handgate and keep a fence on the left over rolling sheep pasture. The path eventually swings right to cross a track through 2 gates (blue arrows). Cross a field along the line indicated by the second arrow, to reach the Hartshorne road through another handgate by a lake.*

3. *Turn right along this minor yet often busy road. In $\frac{1}{4}$ mile, 30 metres before reaching a brick-built bridge, turn right up a track. Climb past a bungalow on the right to skirt woodland. Cross a stile by a gate and continue between fences to another stile between a gate and a yew tree. Follow the clear woodland track until it descends to meet a road on the left, leading to a house ahead.*

4. *Swing right here, following the track as it climbs towards woodland. At the top of the slope, the route continues between fences, then crosses gallops and passes more woodland on the left before dipping to pass between two lakes. Bretby Hall now comes into view ahead. The route climbs the track with the hall on the left. At the top, turn left (ignore stile straight on) and follow a crosstrack through a gateway to reach the main drive.*

5. *Turn right down this drive. (Beware of traffic.) Follow the drive as far as a stile on the right near a power pole. A well-used footpath crosses the fields over 3 stiles to reach Bretby village green and the start.*

1698. She was most impressed by the gardens: 'In one garden there are 3 fountaines wherin stands great statues, each side on their pedistalls is a Dial, one for the sun, the other a Clock which by the water worke is moved and strikes the hours and chimes the quarters, and when they please play Lillibolero on the Chimes – all this I heard when I was there.'

Refreshments
There is no pub at Bretby. Why not picnic on the green or drive the short distance to Foremark Reservoir and eat overlooking the water?

Bretby Hall

Ticknall and Calke Park

Outline

Ticknall – Poker's Leys – Calke Park – Calke Abbey – Ticknall.

Summary

Apart from two short stretches of easy road walking, this route follows public footpaths through a gentle pastoral landscape of fields, woodland fringes and the spacious parkland surrounding Calke Abbey. The concluding stages of the route provide yet more variety in the form of flooded claypits, shaded by clumps of trees, and the stroll through the interesting village of Ticknall sets the seal on a memorable walk.

Attractions

'The place where time stood still' was the phrase used to describe Calke Abbey when it first opened to the public in 1989. From the time of its building, in 1703, until it was given to the National Trust in 1985, Calke was Derbyshire's secret stately home. A splendid mansion, set in over 750 acres of park, nestling in a hollow close to the Leicestershire border. Its owners, the Harpur-Crewes, were content to let the outside world pass them by.

All that has now changed. The park, with its venerable old oaks, herd of deer and delightful ponds, can be enjoyed either by walking from Ticknall or from the official car park, while the Abbey – a misleading name, for no trace of the 12th century Augustinian abbey remains – can be toured at leisure, together with its gardens and stables, and full use made of the excellent public facilities.

The first and last stages of the walk reveal something of the industrial history of the area. Until Victorian times, both lime and clay were obtained to the south of Ticknall and the mouth of an old tramway tunnel connecting the workings with the village is passed soon after the start of the walk. Children may well enjoy peeping along the low straight tunnel, which is remarkably well preserved. On the last mile or so back to Ticknall, the route passes a cluster of old clay pits, now reclaimed by nature and half-hidden by mature trees. These add to the other rich wildlife habitats encountered on the route.

Despite being on a main road, Ticknall retains much of its attractive character. Bricks and pottery were once made here and many of its stone and brick cottages are as picturesque as any in the region. Notice the handsome bridge, which once carried a tramway from the clay pits, also the Harpur almshouses of 1772 and the tiny cone-roofed lock-up, a miniature gaol in which felons were temporarily imprisoned.

Sharp-eyed children may spot the two fragments of a ruined building standing in the churchyard. These are all that remains of the old parish church, which was

Continued on page 74

Route 16

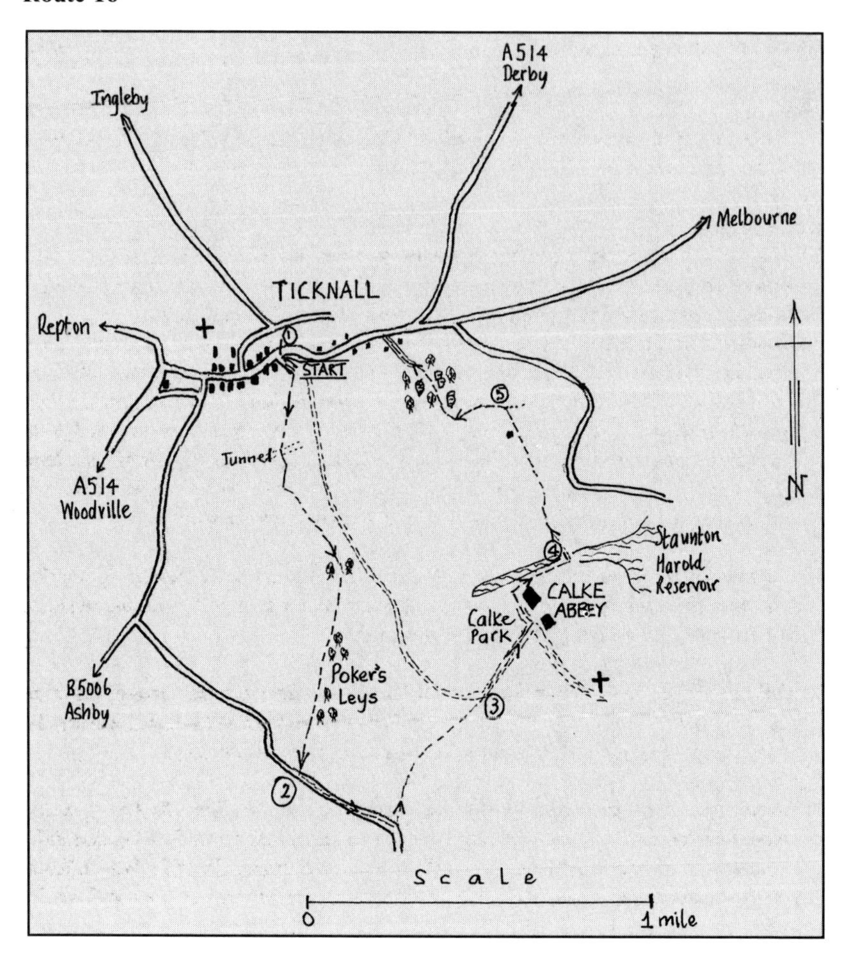

A514
Derby
Ingleby
Melbourne
TICKNALL
Repton
START
Tunnel
A514
Woodville
Staunton
Harold
Reservoir
CALKE
ABBEY
Calke
Park
Poker's
Leys
B5006
Ashby
Scale
0
1 mile
N

Route 16

Ticknall and Calke Park — $4\frac{3}{4}$ miles

Start

Ticknall, a village on the A514, 5 miles SW of Swarkestone. Parking available in village off main road (OS Landranger Sheet 128. GR 353239).

Route

1. *The walk commences from the entrance to Banton's Lane, 60 metres from the Wheel Inn, on the A514, almost opposite the junction with the minor road to Ingleby. Follow the lane to its end and go through a kissing-gate. Turn right to skirt woodland on the left to a stile in a fence just beyond the tramway tunnel entrance. From here, a clear track passes right of a pond. After a footpath from the right joins the track via a stile, swing left across the park towards the drive before veering right to a stile by a metal gate. Descend a field with first a wood, then a wall, on the left, to enter and leave a wood over stiles. Continue, following a long stretch of woodland (Poker's Leys) on the left. Cross a stile at the far end and go over a field, passing to the left of the right-hand power pole to reach a road over a stile.*

2. *Turn left along the road as far as a right-hand bend. Leave the road here by turning left through a stile by a gate to follow a track. Cross a stile and continue, to reach the drive to Calke Abbey through a handgate.*

3. *Follow the drive as it swings into the car park. The route continues through a gate in the wall on the left. Swing right alongside the wall and descend to Mere Pond by the steps. Keep the pond on the left as far as a dam, which is crossed.*

4. *Go through a handgate and climb by the deer fence on the right. At the top of the slope, turn left and, in 40 metres, right through a gate in the wall. Go left, then right (yellow arrow) to cross a field diagonally towards a cottage. Cross 2 stiles and keep a hedge/wall on the left at first, later on the right, to join a track coming in from the right.*

5. *Turn left along the track, which winds through overgrown clay pits, eventually becoming a road, leading to the A514. Turn left along the pavement back into Ticknall and the start.*

demolished at the time of the opening of the present church in the 1840s. Happily, some monuments from the old building were transferred to the new one, the spire of which is a local landmark.

Refreshments
Calke Abbey restaurant. Staff of Life and Wheel Inn, Ticknall. Alternatively, the viewpoint overlooking Staunton Harold reservoir, $\frac{3}{4}$ mile NE of Calke church, is a good place for a picnic.

Calke Abbey

Useful Information

Routes in order of difficulty

Easy short walks (less than 4 miles)
Route 4 – Cubley and Hungry Bentley
Route 5 – Longford village and park
Route 8 – Shipley Country Park
Route 11 – Elvaston Castle Country Park
Route 12 – Shardlow

More strenuous walks (less than 4 miles)
Route 1 – Alport Height
Route 2 – Carsington Water
Route 15 – Bretby village and park

Easy longer walks (more than 4 miles)
Route 7 – Ecclesbourne Valley
Route 13 – Barrow and Swarkestone
Route 16 – Ticknall and Calke Park

More strenuous longer walks (more than 4 miles)
Route 3 – Shirley and Osmaston
Route 6 – Doveridge, Waldley and Somersal Herbert
Route 9 – Around Morley
Route 10 – Dale Abbey and Locko Park
Route 14 – Ingleby and Foremark

Public transport facilities

Although it is assumed that most families will travel to the starting place of the walks by car, several of the routes are within reach by public transport.

Busline – 0332 292200 – is a telephone service providing information on bus services throughout Derbyshire.
Other useful numbers: Derby City Transport: 0332 754433
Trent Buses, Uttoxeter Road, Derby: 0332 43201

For information on rail services, ring Derby Railway Station: 0332 32051

Historic buildings open to the public

Calke Abbey and Park near Ticknall. National Trust. Early 18th century house in 750-acre park.
Kedleston Hall near Derby. Curzon family seat. 18th century hall and parkland. National Trust.
Melbourne Hall Melbourne. 17th century hall and gardens.
Sudbury Hall Sudbury, near Uttoxeter. National Trust. 17th century house with Museum of Childhood and lakeside picnic area.
Tutbury Castle near Burton-on-Trent. 12th century ruined fortress.

Museums

Aeropark East Midlands Airport, Castle Donington. Visitor centre with play area.
Bass Museum Burton-on-Trent. Museum of brewing with horse-drawn tours.
Carriage Museum Darley Dale, Matlock. Working stables and horse-drawn coach tours.
Cromford Mill near Matlock. Sir Richard Arkwright's first mill, canal and pumphouse. Mill exhibition. High Peak Junction workshops.
Derby Industrial Museum Silk Mill, Full Street. Rolls Royce aero engine and railway engineering exhibitions.
Derby Museum & Art Gallery The Strand. Civil and military history, natural history and porcelain. Children's holiday activities.
Donington Collection Castle Donington. Racing car museum.
Elvaston Castle Museum Elvaston Castle Country Park. Rural crafts and agricultural machinery.
Erewash Museum Ilkeston. Local history collection displayed in Victorian setting.
Heritage Brewery Museum Burton-on-Trent. Working museum set in old brewery complex.
John King's Workshop Museum Pinxton near Alfreton. History of coalmining.
Museum of Childhood Sudbury Hall, near Uttoxeter. (See Sudbury Hall under Historic Buildings.)
National Stone Centre Wirksworth. Geology, archaeology and quarrying. Trails and gem panning.
National Tramway Museum Crich, near Matlock. Open air working museum. Tram rides and exhibitions.
Peak District Mining Museum Matlock Bath. Lead mining history.
Temple Mine Matlock Bath. Reconstructed lead and fluorspar mine.
Uttoxeter Heritage Centre Carter Street. 17th century timber-framed building housing local history exhibits.
Wirksworth Heritage Centre Market Place. Local industries and crafts.

Stoat

Parks and Country Centres

Allestree Park near Derby. Over 300 acres of scenic parkland. Children's animal corner.
Alton Towers near Uttoxeter. Famous leisure park.
American Adventure Theme Park Ilkeston.
Elvaston Castle Country Park near Derby. 200 acres of park, lake and woodland. Information Centre, trails and exhibitions.
Gulliver's Kingdom Theme Park Matlock Bath. Rides, fairground and adventure fort.
Heights of Abraham and Cable Car Matlock Bath. Cable car rides and cavern tours. Views, play and picnic areas.
High Tor Grounds Matlock Bath. Roman caves, views, play and picnic areas.
Ilam Country Park near Ashbourne. Over 80 acres of park and woodland. Information Centre.
Markeaton Park 200 acres of parkland with lake. Play and picnic areas.
Riber Castle Wildlife Park near Matlock. Rare breeds of birds and mammals. Children's playground and picnic area.
Shipley Country Park near Heanor. 600 acres of woodland, parkland and lakes. Visitor Centre, trails and exhibitions.

Old Dove Bridge, Doveridge (Route 6)

Other Places of Interest

Bentley Fields Open Farm Alkmonton, Longford. Working farm with rare breeds. Play area and field trail.
Carsington Reservoir near Wirksworth. Vast new reservoir. Visitor Centre and adventure playground.
Crich Stand Sherwood Foresters Regimental Memorial, near Cromford. Viewpoint with picnic area.
Dale Abbey near Derby. Remnant of 12th century abbey. Ancient church and hermitage.
Foremark Reservoir near Repton. Walks linking car parks. Waterfowl. Picnic and play areas.
Matlock Bath Aquarium North Parade. Assorted aquaria with tropical and freshwater fish.
Middleton Top Engine House near Middleton-by-Wirksworth. Visitor Centre and restored 19th century steam winding engine.
Midland Railway Centre Butterley, near Ripley. Steam locomotives, train rides and narrow gauge railway.
Peak Rail Matlock station. Preservation Society project to re-open line linking Darley Dale and Matlock stations.
Staunton Harold Reservoir near Melbourne. 200 acre reservoir. Picnic areas and nature reserve.
Staunton Harold Hall grounds, lake, church, tea- and craftshops.

Tourist Information Centres

Ashbourne: 13 Market Place, DE6 1EU. (0335) 43666.
Burton-upon-Trent: Unit 40, Octagon Centre, New Street. (0283) 516609.
Derby: The Market Place, Derby. (0332) 255802.
Matlock Bath: The Pavilion, DE4 3NR. (0629) 55082.

Other useful addresses

Derby City Council: The Council House, Corporation Street.
Leisure Services: Roman House, Friargate.
Derbyshire County Council: County Offices, Matlock.
Derbyshire Wildlife Trust: Elvaston Castle, Derby, DE7 3EP.
National Trust: Clumber Park Stableyard, Worksop, Notts.
Peak Park Planning Board: Aldern House, Baslow Road, Bakewell.

Golden Gates, Elvaston (Route 11)

THE FAMILY WALKS SERIES

Family Walks on Anglesey. Laurence Main. ISBN 0 907758 665.
Family Walks in Berkshire & North Hampshire. Kathy Sharp. ISBN 0 907758 371.
Family Walks around Bristol, Bath & the Mendips. Nigel Vile. ISBN 0 907758 193.
Family Walks around Cardiff & the Valleys. Gordon Hindess. ISBN 0 907758 541.
Family Walks in Cheshire. Chris Buckland. ISBN 0 907758 290.
Family Walks in Cornwall. John Caswell. ISBN 0 907758 55X.
Family Walks in the Cotswolds. Gordon Ottewell. ISBN 0 907758 150.
Family Walks on Exmoor & the Quantocks. John Caswell. ISBN 0 907758 460.
Family Walks in South Gloucestershire. Gordon Ottewell. ISBN 0 907758 339.
Family Walks in Gower. Amanda Green. ISBN 0 907758 630.
Family Walks in Hereford and Worcester. Gordon Ottewell. ISBN 0 907758 207.
Family Walks on the Isle of Wight. Laurence Main. ISBN 0 907758 568.
Family Walks in North West Kent. Clive Cutter. ISBN 0 907758 363.
Family Walks in the Lake District. Barry McKay. ISBN 0 907758 401.
Family Walks in Mendip, Avalon & Sedgemoor. Nigel Vile. ISBN 0 907758 41X.
Family Walks in the New Forest. Nigel Vile. ISBN 0 907758 606.
Family Walks in Oxfordshire. Laurence Main. ISBN 0 907758 38X.
Family Walks in the Dark Peak. Norman Taylor. ISBN 0 907758 169.
Family Walks in the White Peak. Norman Taylor. ISBN 0 907758 096.
Family Walks in South Derbyshire. Gordon Ottewell. ISBN 0 907758 614.
Family Walks in South Shropshire. Marian Newton. ISBN 0 907758 304.
Family Walks in Snowdonia. Laurence Main. ISBN 0 907758 320.
Family Walks in the Staffordshire Peaks and Potteries. Les Lumsdon. ISBN 0 907758 347.
Family Walks around Stratford & Banbury. Gordon Ottewell. ISBN 0 907758 495.
Family Walks in Suffolk. C J Francis. ISBN 0 907758 649.
Family Walks around Swansea. Raymond Humphreys. ISBN 0 907758 622.
Family Walks in the Teme Valley. Camilla Harrison. ISBN 0 907758 452.
Family Walks in Three Peaks & Malham. Howard Beck. ISBN 0 907758 428
Family Walks in Mid Wales. Laurence Main. ISBN 0 907758 274.
Family Walks in the North Wales Borderlands. Gordon Emery. ISBN 0 907758 509.
Family Walks in Warwickshire. Geoff Allen. ISBN 0 907758 533.
Family Walks in the Weald of Kent & Sussex. Clive Cutter. ISBN 0 907758 517.
Family Walks in Wiltshire. Nigel Vile. ISBN 0 907758 215.
Family Walks in the Wye Valley. Heather & Jon Hurley. ISBN 0 907758 266.
Family Walks in the North Yorkshire Dales. Howard Beck. ISBN 0 907758 525.
Family Walks in South Yorkshire. Norman Taylor. ISBN 0 907758 258.
Family Walks in West Yorkshire. Howard Beck. ISBN 0 907758 436.

The publishers welcome suggestions for further titles in this series; and will be pleased to consider manuscripts relating to Derbyshire from new or established authors.

Scarthin Books of Cromford, in the Peak District, are also leading second-hand and antiquarian booksellers, and are eager to purchase specialised material, both ancient and modern.
Contact Dr D. J. Mitchell, 0629-823272.